THE CREDO SERIES

VOLUMES ALREADY PUBLISHED

THE CREDO SERIES

PLANNED AND EDITED BY
RUTH NANDA ANSHEN

Board of Editors

LIVING IN
A WORLD
REVOLUTION

My Encounters with History

BY

HANS KOHN

 A TRIDENT PRESS BOOK
NEW YORK 1964

Prepared under the supervision of
POCKET BOOKS, INC.

LIBRARY OF CONGRESS CATALOG NUMBER: 63-18546
PUBLISHED SIMULTANEOUSLY IN THE UNITED STATES AND CANADA
BY TRIDENT PRESS
MANUFACTURED IN THE UNITED STATES OF AMERICA

To Yetty, companion of my life, and to our grandchildren Gail, Peter, Sheila, and Robert

Sic rerum summa novatur
Semper, et inter se mortales mutua vivunt.
Augescunt aliae gentes, aliae minuuntur,
Inque brevi spatio mutantur saecla animantum
Et quasi cursores vitae lampada tradunt.

Thus the sum of things is ever being replenished,
And mortals live one and all by give and take.
Some peoples wax and others wane,
And in a short space all living things are changed,
And like runners hand on the torch of life.

Lucretius (*De rerum natura,* II, 75)

CONTENTS

THE CREDO SERIES

Its Meaning and Function   **xi**

BY RUTH NANDA ANSHEN

CONTENTS

THE CREDO SERIES

Its Meaning and Function

The Credo Series suggests that an epoch has come to an end, an epoch in which our best knowledge has been dimmed with boredom or darkened by destruction. We have felt for too long that this must be the very nature of life; this is the way life is, and to such a degree that life has consented to shrink from its own terrors, leading us to a deep apostasy of the heart and a crucifixion of our natural aspiration for experience and growth.

The absolute has surrendered to the relative. Our era of relativity, however, whether in science or in morals, does not allow us to assume that relativity implies an absence of ground to stand on, and therefore a relaxation of all effort toward foundations. "There is no firm ground," the dominant malaise of our time, this acceptance of non-finality, summons us to a heightened task. For the failure of formulated absolutes leaves the absolute requirement to evaluate again that uncaptured reality which contains and guides the total meaning of our existence.

The Credo Series hopes to unlock a consciousness that at first sight may seem to be remote but is proved on acquaintance to be surprisingly immediate since it shows the need to reconcile the life of action with the life of contemplation, practice with principle, thought with feeling, knowledge with being, and work, no longer a form of punishment as in the Judeo-Christian tradition, but accepted as a way toward the growth and realization of the self in all its plenitude. For the whole meaning of self lies within the observer and its shadow is cast naturally on the object observed. The fragmentation of man from his work, the being of man into an eternal and temporal half, results in an estrangement of man from his creative source, from his fellows and from himself.

The symbol of *The Credo Series* is the Eye of Osiris. It is the inner Eye. Man sees in two ways: with his physical eyes, in an empirical sensing or *seeing* by direct observation, and also by an indirect envisaging. He possesses in addition to his two sensing eyes a single, image-making, spiritual and intellectual Eye. And it is the *in-sight* of this inner Eye that purifies and makes sacred our understanding of the nature of things, for that which was shut fast has been opened by the command of the inner Eye. And we become aware that to believe is to see.

Thus, it is suggested, there may be born a sharpened vision, which comes from seeing reality as the incarnation of associations and affinities with something beyond the visible self. For it is our hope to show the human relevance of ideas, the ways in which knowledge can help us to live in the immediate and real world by pointing to the confluence of man and his vocation, of subject and object, by reverencing the curious and mysterious metabolism between man and matter, the sacred nexus between the person and his work, and by asking whether the freedom now released through the creative energies of mankind will bring salvation or destruction, the answer to which will depend upon the aims we cherish.

The Credo Series submits that the universe itself is a vast entity where man will be lost if it does not converge in the person; for material forces or energies, or impersonal ideals, or scientifically objectified learning are meaningless without their relevance for human life and their power to disclose, even in the dark tendencies of man's nature, a law transcending man's arbitrariness.

For the personal is a far higher category than the abstract universal. Personality itself is an emotional, not an intellectual, experience, and the greatest achievement of knowledge is to combine the personal within a larger unity, just as in the higher stages of development the parts that make up the whole acquire greater and greater independence and individuality within the context of the whole. Reality itself is the harmony which gives to the component particulars of a thing the equilibrium of the whole. And while physical observations are ordered with direct reference to the experimental conditions, we have in sensate experience to do with separate observations whose correlation can only be indicated by their belonging to the wholeness of mind.

It is our endeavor to show that man has reached a turning point in consciousness, that his relationship with his creative self demands a clarification that can widen and deepen his understanding of the nature of reality. Work is made for man, not man for work. This Series hopes to demonstrate the sacramental character of work, which is more easily achieved when the principal objects of our attention have taken on a symbolic form that is generally recognized and accepted: in other words, when there is an established iconography relating to the meaningful interpretation of man and his vocation. This suggests a "law" in the relationship of a person and his chosen discipline:

that it is valuable only when the spiritual, the creative, life
is strong enough to insist on some expression through
symbols. For no work can be based on material, technological or physical aspirations alone.

The human race is now entering upon a new phase of
evolutionary progress, a phase in which, impelled by the
forces of evolution itself, it must converge upon itself and
convert itself into one single human organism dominated
by a reconciliation of knowing and being in their inner
unity and destined to make a qualitative leap into a higher
form of consciousness that would transcend and comple-
ment individual consciousness as we know it, or otherwise
destroy itself. For the entire universe is one vast field,
potential for incarnation, and achieving incandescence
here and there of reason and spirit. What to some is mystery and inscrutability, to others symbolizes and declares
the very nature of the cosmic process. And in the whole
world of *quality* with which category by the nature of our
minds we necessarily make contact, we here and there
apprehend pre-eminent value. This can be achieved only
if we recognize that we are unable to focus our attention
on the particulars of a whole without diminishing our
comprehension of the whole, and of course conversely, we
can focus on the whole only by diminishing our comprehension of the particulars which constitute the whole.

This Series is designed to present a kind of intellectual
autobiography of each author, to portray the nature and
meaning of the creative process for the creator and to
show the relevance of his work to the feelings and aspirations of the man of flesh and bone. This Series endeavors
to reflect also the influence of the work on the man and on
society and to point to the freedom, or lack of freedom, to
choose and pursue one profession rather than another.

It attempts to emphasize that the creator in any realm must surrender himself to a passionate pursuit of the hidden meaning of his labors, guided by deep personal intimations of an as yet undiscovered reality.

These volumes endeavor to indicate that it is impossible to know what constitutes a good society unless we know what defines a good individual. The self is determined by the values according to which it subordinates and integrates the rest of its values. If the values be transient, so is the self. If the values be dispersed and incoherent, so is the self. If they are organic and integrated, so is the self. The unity of human personality is its soundness. The unified self cannot be understood in terms of its constituent parts as dissected away from each other. So that finally what we see and what we do are no more and no less than what we are.

It is the effort of *The Credo Series* to define the new reality in which the estrangement of man and his work, resulting in the self-estrangement in man's existence, is overcome. This new reality is born through the reconciliation of what a man *knows* with what a man *is*. Being itself in all its presuppositions and implications can only be understood through the totality, through wholeness. St. Paul, who, like Isaiah before him, went into the marketplace not to secularize truth but to proclaim it, taught man that the "new creation" could be explained only by conquering the demonic cleavages, the destructive split, in soul and cosmos. And that fragmentation always destroys a unity, produces a tearing away from the source and thereby creates disunity and isolation. The fruit can never be separated from the tree. The Tree of Life can never be disjoined from the Tree of Knowledge for both have *one and the same* root. And if man allows himself to fall into

isolation, if he seeks to maintain a self segregated from the
totality of which he is a necessary part, if he chooses to
remain asunder, unrelated to the original context of all
created things in which he too has his place—including
his own labors—then this act of apostasy bears fruit in the
demiurgical presumption of *magic,* a form of animism in
which man seeks an authority of the self, placing himself
above the law of the universe by attempting to separate
the inseparable. He thus creates an unreal world of false
contexts after having destroyed or deserted the real. And
in this way the method of analysis, of scientific objectivity,
which is good and necessary in its right place, is endowed
with a destructive power when it is allowed to usurp a
place for which it is not fitted.

The naturalist principle that man is the measure of all
things has been shattered more than ever in our own age
by the question "What is the measure of man?" Post-
modern man is more profoundly perplexed about the
nature of man than his ancestors were. He is on the verge
of spiritual and moral insanity. He does not know who he
is. And having lost the sense of who and what he is, he
fails to grasp the meaning of his fellow man, of his vocation, and of the nature and purpose of knowledge itself.
For what is not understood cannot be known. And it is
this cognitive faculty which is frequently abrogated by the
"scientific" theory of knowledge, a theory that refuses to
recognize the existence of comprehensive entities as distinct from their particulars. The central act of knowing is
indeed that form of comprehension which is never absent
from any process of knowing and is finally its ultimate
sanction.

Science itself acknowledges as real a host of entities that
cannot be described completely in materialistic or mecha-

nistic terms, and it is this transcendence out of the domain of science into a region from which science itself can be appraised that *The Credo Series* hopes to expose. For the essence of the ebb and flow of experience, of sensations, the richness of the immediacy of directly apprehended knowledge, the metaphysical substance of what assails our being, is the very act itself of sensation and affection and therefore must escape the net of rational analysis, yet is intimately related to every cognitive act. It is this increasing intellectual climate that is calling into birth once more the compelling Socratic questions, "What is the purpose of life, the meaning of work?" "What is man?" Plato himself could give us only an indirect answer: "Man is declared to be that creature who is constantly in search of himself, a creature who at every moment of his existence must examine and scrutinize the conditions of his existence. He is a being in search of meaning."

Theory and life always go together. An organic conception of man and his work, man and society, man and the universe, is portrayed in First Corinthians 12 when Paul relates the famous story of the strife that once broke out between the parts of the human body. They refused to fulfill their special functions within the organism until they finally learned that they are all parts of one body and can exist and function only as such. For they all breathe together. And by so doing subordinate themselves to the presentation of the whole body. What may be an explanation of organic life in the human body may be transferred to the life in the universe and to the relationship between the interior and the exterior, for all is permeated by the life-giving creative power—by unity.

The authors in this endeavor are aware that man in the twentieth century finds himself in the greatest revolution since the discovery of agriculture. They show, each in his own way, that part of the meaning of our present turmoil may indeed lie in its being the means to reconcile thought and action, to overcome the parochialism of dogmas that only isolate man from man and man from the implicit meaning of his chosen profession. Our effort is to create an image of man intelligible and unitary, a microcosmic mirror of the greater macrocosm of which he is a part and in which he has his legitimate place in relation to the whole. For even the extraordinary successes of scientific predictions, the fruits of man's ingenuity in inventing the scientific method, seem comprehensible only on the basis that the human mind possesses an inherent logic closely parallel with the structure of the external world itself.

The very interdependence of the observer and the participant can no longer be ignored as part of the essential value of things. To take a definitive example from modern cosmology, it is challenging indeed to note that there is a most unusual connection between the existence of stars and the laws that govern the atomic nuclei. Emphasis is placed upon the existence, not the properties, of stars. For everyone expects the properties of stars and atomic nuclei to be related. It is the *connection* with the *existence* of stars that is so reassuring—and indeed surprising.

From this it is evident that there is present in the universe a *law* applicable to all nature including man and his work. Life itself then is seen to be a creative process elaborating and maintaining *order* out of the randomness of matter, endlessly generating new and unexpected structures and properties by building up associations that qualitatively transcend their constituent parts. This is not to diminish the importance of "scientific objectivity." It is, however, to say that the mind possesses a quality that cannot be isolated or known exclusively in the sense of objective knowledge. For it consists in that elusive humanity in us, our self, that knows. It is that inarticulate awareness that includes and *comprehends* all we know. It consists in the irreducible active voice of man and is recognized only in other things, only when the circle of consciousness closes around its universe of events.

The experience of the modern mind has been expressed in terms of conflict produced by false dualisms, disruption, self-destruction, meaninglessness, purposelessness and desperation. This character of our time has found its expression in literature, in art, in existential philosophy, in some forms of natural science, in political demonologies, and is explored in the psychology of the unconscious. Our authors hope to indicate that through a quickening of awareness man can overcome this dualism and can rise to face the meaning of life and work, keeping his mind and energies awake at full stretch. Such knowledge—that form of knowledge which cannot be disjoined from being—will enable man to embrace life with passion and to work with devotion. It will enable him to absorb experience with his whole nature and thereby to fill a want that is satisfied neither by action alone nor by thought alone. This unity of *being* and *doing* has a justifiable claim to be called a form of enchantment since through it men, who might otherwise give in to the malice of circumstances and conditions, find their old powers revived or new powers stirring within them, and through these life is sustained, renewed and fulfilled.

Man is now confronting himself with the compelling need to create an organic identification between what he *is* and what he *does*. For only in this way can the threat of conformism and the treachery of abstraction, the plight of the modern mind, be conquered. This split, inherited from the seventeenth century, between the transitive and the intransitive, between the creator and the process of creativity, has blunted man's appetite for experience. Language itself in our time has failed because man has forgotten that it is the mother of thought, because of its analytical emphasis and thus lacks ready means to convey associations, emotional or imaginative, that cluster around a subject and give to it a distinctive personal significance. In other words, the symbols by which man lives and has his being, that "tacit coefficient"* of articulate knowledge that is unanalyzable, now knocks at the portals of consciousness waiting to be admitted. For human nature loses its most precious quality when it is robbed of its sense of things beyond, unexplored and yet insistent.

The Credo Series belongs to those ideas that are intuitively conceived and that originate in spheres of a spiritual order and surprise thought, as it were, compelling it to transform its inherited notions conformably with its enlarged vision of the nature of things. It is as though the authors of the Series were recovering this reality out of a memory of a lost harmony, a memory latent in the soul and not distilled from the changing things of mere physical observation. In this way the inner unity of the known and the knower may be preserved, and the almost mythic intuition of reality thereby related to its conceptual and rational forms of expression. For man, unlike a machine, is an organism existing as an end in itself. He *is* the system on which causal explanations are based and to which they have to return; he *is* a historically existent whole, a four-

---

* See the classical work, *Personal Knowledge*, by Michael Polanyi for an enlarged meaning of the nature of reality. (Chicago University Press, 1958.)

dimensional entity, and not merely an abstraction from which statements about phenomena are deducible under the guise of eternity.

Our hope is to point to a new dimension of morality—not that of constraint and prohibition but a morality that lies as a fountainhead within the human soul, a morality of aspiration to spiritual experience. It suggests that necessity is laid upon us to infer entities that are not observed and are not observable. For an unseen universe is necessary to explain the seen. The flux is seen, but to account for its structure and its nature we infer particles of various kinds to serve as the vertices of the changing patterns, placing less emphasis on the isolated units and more on the structure and nature of relations. The process of knowing involves an immaterial becoming, an immaterial identification, and finally, knowledge itself is seen to be a dependent variable of immateriality. And somewhere along this spiritual pilgrimage man's pure observation is relinquished and gives way to the deeper experience of awe, for there can be no explanation of a phenomenon by searching for its origin but only by discerning its immanent law—this quality of transcendence that abides even in matter itself.

The present situation in the world and the vast accretion of knowledge have produced a serious anxiety, which may be overcome by re-evaluating the character, kinship, logic and operation of man in relation to his work. For work implies goals and intimately affects the person performing the work. Therefore the correlation and relatedness of ideas, facts and values that are in perpetual interplay could emerge from these volumes as they point to the inner synthesis and organic unity of man and his labors. For though no labor alone can enrich the person, no enrichment can be achieved without absorbing and intense labor. We then experience a unity of faith, labor and grace which prepares the mind for receiving a truth from sources over which it has no control. This is especially true since the great challenge of our age arises out of man's inventions in relation to his life.

Thus *The Credo Series* seeks to encourage the perfection not only of man's works but also and above all the fulfillment of himself as a person. And so we now are summoned to consider not only man in the process of development as a human subject but also his influence on the object of his investigation and creation. Observation alone is interference. The naïve view that we can observe any system and predict its behavior without altering it by the very act of observation was an unjustified extrapolation from Newton's *Celestial Mechanics*. We can observe the moon or even a satellite and predict its behavior without appreciably interfering with it, but we cannot do this with an amoeba, far less with a man and still less with a society of men. It is the heart of the question of the nature of work itself. If we regard our labors as a process of shaping or forming, then the fruits of our labors play the part of a mold by which we ourselves are shaped. And this means, in the preservation of the identity of the knower and the known, that cognition and generation, that is, creation, though in different spheres, are nevertheless alike.

It is hoped that the influence of such a Series may help to overcome the serious bifurcation of function and meaning and may show that the extraordinary crisis through which the world is passing can be fruitfully met by recognizing that knowledge has not been completely dehumanized and has not totally degenerated into a mere notebook overcrowded with formulas that few are able to understand or apply.

For mankind is now engaged in composing a new theme. Potentiality and actuality possess a profound and abiding intimacy. Life refuses to be embalmed alive. Life cannot abjure life; nothing that lives is born out of nothingness. But nothing, either, can preserve its form against the ceaseless flux of being. Life never manifests itself in negative terms. And our hope lies in drawing from every category of work a conviction that nonmaterial values can be discovered in positive, affirmative, visible things. The estrangement between the temporal and nontemporal man is coming to an end, community is inviting communion and a vision of the human condition more worthy of man is engendered, connecting ever more closely the creative mind with the currents of spiritual energy, which breaks for us the bonds of habit and keeps us in touch with the permanence of being in all its plenitude through our work.

And as, long ago, the Bearers of Bread were succeeded by the Bearers of Torches, so now, in the immediacies of life, it is the image of man and his vocation that can rekindle the high passion of humanity in its quest for light. Refusing to divorce work from life or love from knowledge, it is action, it is passion that enhances our being.

We live in an expanding universe and also in the moral infinite of that other universe, the universe of man. And along the whole stretched arc of this universe we may see that extreme limit of complicity where reality seems to shape itself within the work man has chosen for his realization. Work then becomes not only a way of knowledge, it becomes even more a way of life—of life in its totality. For the last end of every maker is himself.

"And the places that have been desolate for ages shall be built in thee: thou shalt raise up the foundations of generation and generation; and thou shalt be called the repairer of the fences, turning the paths into rest."*

—RUTH NANDA ANSHEN

* Isaiah, 58:12

LIVING IN A WORLD REVOLUTION:
My Encounters With History

I

YOUTH IN HISTORIC PRAGUE

I WAS BORN IN Central Europe at the beginning of the last decade of the nineteenth century. At the age of twenty-two, when I had just finished my courses at the University, history and my life took an unexpected turn: the First World War broke out. That conflict changed, almost beyond recognition, the order and prospects of my personal life, of my homeland, of the nations of Europe, and of peoples everywhere.

The preceding decades had been an era of peace and security. Even today, many remember this period as the beautiful sunset of an ordered and cultured society and way of life. And indeed, life was then easy and pleasant for the upper classes of the surviving semifeudal order— the happy few. The pace of technological advance, assuring ever greater comforts, was still relatively slow; the belief in man's perfectibility and in continuous progress were articles of faith not yet beset by doubts; the life of the average citizen was fairly leisurely and relaxed; governmental interference was limited; freedom, though largely for a privileged minority, seemed assured, and at the same time its compass was steadily widening; international intercourse was easy. Under the surface there was longing,

1

among many young people, for far-reaching social and political transformations, but few expected to see their vague hopes realized during their lifetime.

The outbreak of the war changed all this. Its four years formed a much deeper break in modern history than did the twenty-five years of the French Revolution and the Napoleonic Wars. Though the Napoleonic era ushered in profound changes, its impact, on the whole, was confined to the Western world. It barely penetrated beyond the fringes of Western Europe into Russia, Turkey, and Egypt; it was not felt at all in China or Japan, India or Africa. Moreover, the French Revolution proved but a temporary threat to the established order in Europe. It toppled some existing dynastic systems only to end in the restoration of legitimacy. The Bourbons returned; the Habsburgs and Romanovs, though momentarily shaken, seemed little changed. Life in Europe around 1830 was not very different from what it had been in 1780, in its governmental structure, its social attitudes, and in its political and social institutions.

How different was the impact of the First World War! Its repercussions were immediate and permanent, and they were felt all over the globe. In Europe a restoration of the three dynasties which held such a prominent place at the beginning of the twentieth century—the Habsburgs, the Hohenzollerns, the Romanovs—was no longer a serious possibility. In the 1870's, forty-five years after the Bourbons lost the French throne, strong royalist factions in France still worked for the re-establishment of the legitimate monarchy; forty-five years after 1918, a restoration in Central or Eastern Europe, in the very lands which under Metternich and Bismarck had been the stronghold of extreme monarchical conservatism, was unthinkable. The world of the 1960's differs in every respect from that of 1910, in which I grew up, not only in Europe but even more in Asia and Africa. This revolutionary half-century has shaken the world and aroused a demand for equality and human dignity among the subject multitudes who had been neglected or oppressed throughout history; it has annihilated time and distance and has brought together the peoples of all nations. This half-century also coincides with the span of my mature life.

Fate and personal decision combined to make me a dweller in many lands, a *Bürger vieler Welten,* during those years. In my encounters with history, my faith in man's destiny has grown. These seventy years, despite their barbarism and destructiveness, their bitter nationalist struggles, and their repudiation of traditional norms of social and political behavior, have resulted in a better life for most peoples. For this reason, at the climax of this era of revolutionary change and at the twilight of my life, I assent, hopefully and gratefully, to both of them—to the world revolution and to my life.

Yet as I grew up in Prague in the serene years at the turn of the century, my coming encounters with history, with foreign lands and civilizations, and my acceptance of them, would have seemed beyond imagination. Prague was my home, the Austrian monarchy my fatherland, and, not unreasonably, I felt a sentimental loyalty toward both.

Prague is one of the most beautiful cities in Europe. The broad Moldau River, which flows through its midst, is more intimately a part of this lovely capital than is the Danube in Vienna, the Tiber in Rome, or the Thames in London. It affords even lovelier views of green hills, charming gardens, and towering castles than does the

Seine in Paris. On the right bank of the Moldau stands the acropolis, or Vyšehrad, the site of the first settlement of the city. Farther down, on the Moldau's left bank, rises the royal castle of Hradčany, stretching majestically over a broad expanse of the riverbank with the tall spires of the Cathedral of St. Veit rising from one of its wide courtyards.

On both sides of the river, which is dotted with tree-rich islands and spanned by many bridges, lies the oldest part of the city, full of quaint narrow streets, dark archways, and sumptuous doors that lead into quiet courtyards with a Mediterranean flavor; old inns of fascinating charm; magnificent, aristocratic palaces, mostly in the Baroque style; and an abundance of churches, some Baroque, others Gothic, reflecting the two great periods of cultural and artistic pre-eminence in the city's history—the fourteenth and the seventeenth centuries. The streets in this part of Prague, especially those on the left bank which ascend steeply toward the Hradčany and retain an old-fashioned, aristocratic air, were usually deserted after nightfall. These thoroughfares seemed to refuse assimilation into the modern European capital Prague had now become. Many late evenings, as high school and college students, we walked these streets for hours. Their dark walls reverberated with the animated dialogue of Prague's youthful lovers who were familiar with its storied legends and half-hidden passages. Here the past seemed everywhere alive, evoked in rich legends and memories that recalled the city's colorful history; and so the past renewed its sway from generation to generation. In no other city have I felt the reality of the past so pervasive as in Prague in those years before 1914.

Prague had twice in its past held the center stage in European history. The first of these crucial periods occurred in the fourteenth century under Charles IV, the Luxembourgeois prince who transformed the city. Charles had been born in Prague in 1316, was educated at the French court, and spoke five languages. To the kingdom of Bohemia which he inherited, he soon added the possessions of Silesia, Lusatia, and Brandenburg. He also gave new luster to the Bohemian crown by his election as King of Germany in 1346. In 1354 he was crowned King of Italy and Emperor of the Holy Roman Empire. He made Bohemia the most advanced state in Central Europe and Prague the first seat of the new humanism north of the Alps. Charles chose Prague as the seat of the first university in Central Europe—named Charles University, after him—and built many other structures that still commemorate his transformation of the city, among them the oldest stone bridge across the Moldau River, a majestic structure even today, adorned in later years with an imposing array of statues of saints.

The peace and prosperity of Charles IV's reign did not continue under his successors, however. In the fifteenth century, Prague and Bohemia became the stage for the first religious reformation, the Hussite movement, which, in many ways, also anticipated modern nationalism and modern social revolutions. The Hussite Wars devastated Bohemia, but their evocation later, in the age of nationalism, served as a powerful impetus for the awakening of the Czech people.

Jan Hus (1369-1415) was the central figure in this nationalistic challenge to the universal church. A rector and teacher at the University, he also preached his doctrine of Christianity in the vernacular. The steadfastness

and heroism with which Hus suffered his ordeal at the
stake as a heretic—he was condemned to death by the
general Church Council of Constance—aroused his Czech
followers. Under their military leader Jan Žižka (1376-
1424), they established a camp in southwestern Bohemia
to which they gave the biblical name Tabor, so to resist
the crusade proclaimed by the papacy in 1420 "for the
destruction of the Wycliffites, Hussites, and all other here-
tics in Bohemia." Though the Taborites, or extreme Hussites, were defeated, the spirit of Hussitism made Bohemia
a fertile soil for the subsequent spread of the Reformation
in the sixteenth century.

Prague in the early seventeenth century became the·
focal point of the great religious struggle known as the
Thirty Years' War. This devastating conflict broke out in
the city in 1618 and ended there in 1648. Its outcome determined, as far as Bohemia was concerned, the victory
of the Catholic Counter-Reformation under the Habsburgs who had become, in 1526, by the right of inheri-
tance, Kings of Bohemia. The *ecclesia triumphans* found
its architectural expression in the Baroque, the monumental splendor of which was nowhere as gracefully realized as in Prague, Vienna, and some southern German
cities. The Jesuit College of the Clementinum was now
added to the Gothic Carolinum as the joint foundation of
Prague University. As a student I followed the courses in
law and political science in the Carolinum and those in
philosophy and the humanities in the Clementinum, where
the University Library was located. It was an old-fashioned library, staffed by very old, slow-moving attendants
who brought the books from the stacks. The catalogues
were enormous, handwritten, leather-bound folio volumes.
This setting, quite out of step with that of modern Ameri-

can libraries, was nevertheless conducive to many happy hours of quiet reading and research. Though it had none of the collegiate life nor the cloister-like appearance of Oxford or Cambridge, Prague University in those days preserved in its corridors, halls, and chapels something of the character which distinguishes those ancient seats of learning in England.

Prague escaped the fate of other once-important cities, like Venice or Bruges, that later became essentially provincial towns, dreaming of the past. Quite the contrary. At the beginning of the twentieth century, Prague was a great city of about half a million inhabitants, in which one encountered not only history as a record of the past, preserved in monuments and inscriptions, but history in the making—the history of the period in which we lived. Life in Prague was typical of the melancholy sweetness of the twilight of the Habsburg empire and of the bitter conflict of nationalities which dominated the history of Central Europe for nearly a century after 1848. In fact, Prague was the foremost European laboratory for the struggles, tensions, and implications of modern nationalism. Here Germanic and Slavic aspirations met head on, and found their principal battleground. This conflict between Germans and Slavs was, in fact, to spark the two great European wars of the twentieth century. At the same time, this plurality of national civilizations and their clash and competition gave to Prague a cosmopolitan and culturally stimulating character.

For many decades before 1848, the birth date of modern nationalism in Central Europe, Czechs and Germans in Bohemia had lived together fairly peacefully and regarded Bohemia as their common fatherland. At the end of the eighteenth century, Prague had been culturally and socially a predominantly German city. Latin was then the language of university and scholarship, German the language of the well-to-do classes and of the administration, and French the language used by high society. Czech was spoken by the common people, who then did not count for very much. No modern Czech literature existed. Then came a tide of change as rapid as the one which the middle of the twentieth century was to witness in Asia and Africa. In March, 1848, when the winds of the February Revolution in Paris swept into Central Europe and suddenly awakened the peoples there, German and Czech students in Prague collaborated in the interests of constitutional freedom and of the common homeland. Three months later, however, their aroused nationalist fervor changed them into bitter enemies. The first Pan-Slav congress met in Prague for the avowed purpose of safeguarding the position and rights of the Slavs under the Austrian monarchy. The Germans began to speak of the Pan-Slav danger, the specter of which haunted them far more than did the specter of communism which Marx and Engels were evoking at this time. The Czechs saw in the Germans (and the Magyars) the deadly enemies of their national aspirations. From then on the two communities faced each other as foes in a bitter, implacable struggle. The contest was not ended until 1939, when the Germans won a seemingly total victory, only to lose their dominance six years later to the Czechs, who gained the final victory in 1945.

By 1900 Prague had become a predominantly Czech city. German was spoken by only about 5 per cent of the population. However, this small group represented a cultural and economic factor far beyond its numerical strength. Perhaps the intensity of its intellectual and artistic life was so great because it was an upper-class group living out of touch with any popular "masses." For many miles on all sides of Prague the countryside was purely Czech; the farmers, workers, and artisans that one met in Prague were Czech. Yet the German-speaking minority among whom I grew up maintained a fully developed, separate cultural and social life of its own. We did not feel isolated. We felt perfectly at home in Prague and in the Czech countryside around the city. All this was our land, too; we breathed its air and loved its contours.

The reactionary nationalism which began to prevail around the turn of the century (and of which more will be said later) glorified the sturdy peasant with his roots in the soil, and the life of the "people" as the only "natural" condition of man. I do not agree with this attitude. Though I lived happily for long periods in small towns, I always felt at home in cities, particularly in cosmopolitan cities. Their streets offered to me as nourishing a "soil" and certainly as great a fascination as fields, meadows, and pastures. In all the cities I have known, I have experienced nature's beauties—trees, grass, birds singing in the mornings, an evening sky full of stars, winds and clouds above my head. From where we live now, high up in a New York apartment house, we enjoy a sweeping view, as we might from a hilltop. In old cities like Prague there are as many surprises to be encountered at the turnings of streets as in the Alps or the Rocky Mountains. In modern metropolitan centers like New York or London each neighborhood has its own distinct character and flavor.

Thus the German minority did not feel the lack of "roots" in Prague. Our roots were there. We even accepted without much reflection the strange fact that in Prague the two national groups lived strictly separated lives. There was little, if any, social or cultural contact between them. Each had its own schools and universities, theaters and concert halls, sport clubs and cabarets, restaurants and cafés—in all fields of life and activity there reigned a voluntary segregation, a kind of tacitly acknowledged "iron curtain" which separated two worlds living side by side, each one self-contained, scarcely communicating. In few other cities was nationalism as living and all-pervasive a force as in Prague at the beginning of the twentieth century.

This experience of my youth predestined me, so to speak, to develop an awareness of the importance of nationalism. Rationally, the conflict between Germans and Czechs in Bohemia should have been solved by compromise. Economic considerations and geographic reality were in favor of such a solution. In two Austrian provinces—in Moravia, where Czechs and Germans lived together much as they did in Bohemia, and in the small province of Bukovina, which was populated by three nationalities, Ukrainians, Rumanians, and Germans—such compromise solutions were found (as compromise solutions were found after World War II for Trieste and for Cyprus). But in the case of Bohemia such a reconciliation of opposite claims, which would have been in the ultimate interest of both groups and would have assured a common future on a reasonable basis, was frustrated by visions and ambitions carried over from the past—and often from a narrow interpretation of that past—and by the emotions aroused by such visions. History was too powerful to allow common sense to prevail.

II

THE TWILIGHT OF THE HABSBURG MONARCHY

So it was in the Austrian monarchy at the time of my youth, an era which coincided with the final decades of the monarchy's existence. The Austro-Hungarian Empire soon fell victim to the rising tide of nationalism, but its disappearance was no blessing; instead, it left a void that neither satisfied nor appeased the conflicting nationalist aspirations, which only grew in bitterness and destructiveness.

The Habsburg monarchy had acted as a restraining influence over a large area of mixed populations located at the crossroads of Europe, stretching from the Alps to the Carpathian Mountains, from the Elbe and the Vistula to the Adriatic Sea. It was the meeting place of all European civilizations, to which the proximity of the Near East added an exotic note. The great variety of ethnic origins, languages, and historical memories in its population made the Austrian Empire the foremost multinational state in nineteenth-century Europe. And loyalty to the dynasty was the sole unifying, emotional force holding it all together.

When I was young, loyalty to the old emperor was still

11

strong. It was frequently said that Austria would only survive as long as Francis Joseph lived. And, indeed, he had become the living symbol of the Austrian monarchy and of monarchy itself. But in his conservatism, his distrust of new ideas, and his incomprehension of popular movements, he made no effort to use loyalty to the Habsburg dynasty as a symbol around which to create an Austrian idea which would unite his peoples and provide the basis for an enduring loyalty, as did the Swiss idea in a similarly multiethnic and multilingual confederation. Francis Joseph was not strong enough to overcome domineering instincts of the three historically most conscious nationalities of his empire—the Magyars, the Germans, and the Poles—so as to permit the development of a cohesive federation based upon the equality of all nationalities. To achieve this, he would have had to turn from his attachment to an aristocratic past to an imaginative vision of a democratic future. This was beyond him.

Francis Joseph assumed the throne in 1848 and ruled for sixty-eight years, longer even than his contemporary, Queen Victoria. To the youth of my generation he seemed to have been in power forever, to have become the eternal symbol of Austria. His portrait looked down upon us from the walls of all school classrooms and all public buildings. He was familiar to us as a venerable old man with white mustache and white whiskers, a likeness imitated by many of the older civil servants and functionaries throughout the land. Francis Joseph shunned publicity; he sedulously avoided the limelight of modern times in which many of his fellow rulers, such as the German emperor, William II, basked with such relish. His retiring nature made

Francis Joseph something of a remote, almost legendary, figure.*

The beginning of his reign was promising. Under revolutionary pressure the court had allowed a democratically elected parliament to convene. That body's most important decision, and its one lasting achievement, was the complete emancipation of the Austrian peasants. Meeting in the small town of Kremsier, in Moravia, the parliament also adopted a constitution. This constitution of March, 1849, reorganized the Empire, granting autonomy to its various parts and equality to its various nationalities. This constitution was the single occasion at which the several nationalities of the Empire, through their representatives, were able to arrive at the solution of the difficult problem of reconciling the unity of the Empire with the rights and freedom of its component nationalities. Unfortunately, the constitution never went into force.

Five days before the young prince's elevation to the throne, in December, 1848, the prime minister, Prince Felix Schwarzenberg, had declared: "We sincerely and without any reservation want the constitutional monarchy, we want the equality of all citizens before the law and equal rights for all nationalities." At his accession Francis Joseph himself had similarly expressed his "conviction" that "on the basis of genuine liberty, on the basis of the equality of all the nations of the realm and the equality before the law of all citizens and of the participation of all those citizens in legislation, our fatherland will enjoy a resurrection to its old greatness and a new vigor."

---

* An Austrian writer of my generation, Joseph Roth, succeeded in re-creating, in his novel *Radetzkymarsch* (1932), something of the legendary atmosphere of the final decades of the reign of Francis Joseph.

But these promises were not kept. Francis Joseph, who had grown to manhood dominated by his bigoted and ambitious mother, now fell under the spell of Prince Felix Schwarzenberg, a strong-willed and arrogant aristocrat who despised constitutional liberalism and was determined to restore absolutism. Schwarzenberg died prematurely in 1852, but the young Emperor could do no better than follow a weak and vacillating policy, best characterized by the great Austrian poet Franz Grillparzer:

> This is the curse of Habsburg's noble house:
> Halfway to halt, and doubtfully to aim
> At half a deed, with half-considered means.

Though Francis Joseph later became a dutiful constitutional monarch, he never forgot that in 1848 the army had saved the dynasty. His deepest interest and loyalty continued to belong to the army, not in the grandiloquent manner of William II, but with an emphasis on simplicity and austerity, on old-fashioned concepts of duty, honor and politesse.

At the beginning of the twentieth century the image of the young prince of 1848 had long faded into the past. Francis Joseph was now an old man, and soon a very old man, bowed by many domestic tragedies—the estrangement of his beautiful, highly gifted, and beloved wife, whose romantic, artistic temperament was incompatible with his unimaginative sobriety; the execution of his brother Maximilian, short-lived ruler of Mexico; the suicide of his only son, who opposed his father's policy and personality; the assassination of his wife by an Italian anarchist. To my generation, Francis Joseph appeared a lonely figure mellowed by age and suffering.

In 1867 Francis Joseph had granted Austria a constitution and from that time on he adhered, more strictly than Queen Victoria, to the limits imposed by it. That the parliament did not work as it should was not due to obstruction on his part but to the conflicts of nationalities in his realm. Its peoples, not the monarch, stultified the constitutional development of Austria. The most bitter battles were fought over apparently insignificant details: the building of a minority school in some frontier town, the inscription of street names, the rank and order of languages on restaurant menus. Emotional nationalistic issues, not rational economic interests, formed the basis for many conflicts. The Emperor pressed for universal and equal suffrage in the election of the House of Representatives in the hope that the masses would be more interested in social reforms and economic measures than in the nationality struggles. He was mistaken. The masses proved as fervent nationalists as the middle class.

The years 1848 and 1849, as we have seen, marked the first crisis in modern Central European history. A second crisis, one with even more disastrous consequences, rose in 1866 and 1867. Bismarck's victory over the German Confederation in 1866 marked the defeat of liberalism and constitutionalism in the German Empire which he created. A similar misfortune for the future peace of Europe was the Compromise *(Ausgleich)* which the Habsburg monarchy concluded in 1867 with the Magyar gentry of Hungary, a compromise which did not fulfill, as it should have, the legitimate ethnic claims of both the Magyars and the other peoples of Hungary and of the Habsburg monarchy, but instead fulfilled only the historical Magyar claims to a favored position as the dominant group in Hungary.

From that moment on, in the newly created Austro-Hungarian Empire—or Dual Monarchy, as it was also termed—the Hungarian half did not share the progressive, democratic evolution characteristic of the Austrian half. Hungary remained socially an underdeveloped, semifeudal country; its parliamentary elections were mockeries, a perversion of the constitutional machinery in the self-interest of the ruling Magyar class. This situation meant not only the oppression of the Hungarian peasantry but of the minority peoples of Hungary, above all the Slovaks and the Rumanians, who lived in a semicolonial status. Yet the arrogant Magyar ruling class, in their blind drive for power, worked incessantly to undermine the tenuous unity of the monarchy and to establish a completely independent Hungary, based not on the rights and equality of the peoples living there but on the quasi-mythical past of the Crown of St. Stephen, whose function was now reinterpreted to serve the purpose of a modern militant nationalism.

The Kremsier constitution of March, 1849, had foreseen the transformation of the whole monarchy into a federation of equal nationalities. The Compromise of 1867 created instead a dualism with Magyar preponderance. Czech leaders warned in vain against this development. They clearly recognized the implications of the fact that geography had placed them and other peoples like the Magyars and Poles between the Russian and the German colossi in such a way that they could not exist by themselves alone without falling victims to their larger neighbors. Austria's historical task was the unification of these lands for common defense and mutual support. The Czech historian František Palacký sounded the warning in his *The Idea of the Austrian State* (1865): ". . . Dualism in any form whatsoever will prove within not-too-long a time destructive of the whole monarchy." He demanded "that the Austrian government should be neither German nor Magyar, Slav nor Latin, but Austrian in a higher and general sense, which means on the basis of equal justice for all its members. . . . That more than three hundred years ago such different peoples have by free agreements formed the Austrian empire I regard as in no way a small blessing by Divine Providence for all of them. If it had not happened and if each of these peoples had kept its full sovereign rights, in how many and how bloody struggles would they have faced each other during that time! Perhaps some of them might even have perished."

Palacký's forecast proved correct. Half a century after 1867 the Hohenzollern Empire created by Bismarck, the dual Habsburg monarchy, and the domination of the Magyars over subject peoples came to a disastrous end. The dissolution of the Habsburg monarchy—welcomed by many "liberals" without a deeper insight into the nature of Central European nationalism—proved to be no blessing for the peoples involved.

The Constitution promulgated for the Austrian half of the Dual Monarchy on December 21, 1867, stipulated in its Article XIX that "All nationalities have equal rights in the state, and each nationality has an inviolable right to preserve and cultivate its nationality and language. All languages used in the various lands will enjoy equality in schools, offices, and public life, and this equality is recognized by the state." The respect for this Article and the growing liberalization of the administrative practice in Austria allowed the nationalities there, after 1867, a rapid progress in popular education, economic strength, and the growth of a new national consciousness.

Austria (outside Hungary) was at the beginning of the twentieth century on the way to becoming a *Vielvölker-reich*, a truly multinational state. Yet the nationalist groups in Austria, eager for the panoply and power of full sovereignty, and equally eager to achieve a dominant position at the expense of other nationalities, continued to complain and press for special privileges. When the monarchy disintegrated under this pressure, its successor states (Czechoslovakia and Poland, Yugoslavia and Rumania), as well as Italy, revealed themselves as less liberal in their nationality policy than the Austrian monarchy had been in its last decades. The "new" states regarded themselves, in spite of their multiethnic composition, as nation-states, with one nationality "native" to the state and the others being tolerated more or less as unwelcome guests. The new states, on the whole, showed less tolerance, less wisdom, and less restraint than the old monarchy had done. There are today many who remember the last decades of multinational Austria with a feeling of nostalgia. And not only because they were young then.

III

THE FASCINATION OF HISTORY

THE VERY AIR of Prague made me a student of history and of nationalism. In the course of the years this study convinced me that the Hegelian-Marxian concept of history as a rational process underestimated both the irrational, emotional forces that motivate men and the importance of the accidental and the contingent in history. Much Hegelianism survives today in the various forms of nationalism, particularly in the non-English-speaking nations, and Marxism survives in the socialism of the underdeveloped countries. In both cases, this "rationalization" of history has disguised the secularization of a fundamentally religious belief in mankind's salvation through history—that is, man's salvation through his membership in a particular nation or in a particular class in society, which supposedly leads or represents mankind, or is at least of universal importance. This concept of messianically meaningful history was first conceived by the Hebrew prophets and was taken over by Christianity. History thus became a *Heilsgeschichte,* a path to a perfect, or messianic, order, preordained by the will of an all-powerful God, who in his mercy concerns himself above all with his "own" people and by whom, in turn, he is gratefully extolled. Nothing, I have learned, is more dangerous to ethics than this claim by nations or classes for divine approval for their ambitions and deeds.

This concept of the one God in history—and history, in its turn, thus gains unity and meaning by being the manifestation of that one God's will—is among the most important contributions of the Judeo-Christian tradition to Western self-awareness. The eighteenth century detached this religious faith, unknown to the Greeks or Oriental peoples, from its religious roots and transformed it into the certainty of an immanent historical process. Attempts were then made to support it by the rational argument of philosophy or the positivist demonstration of social science. Both—philosophy and social science—reached their supreme and superb self-assurance in Hegel and Marx, a feeling very much in accord with the character of the period, typified by man's confident self-reliance.

But Hegel and Marx and their disciples overestimated the inevitability of history. History became the world court, and historical success a product of alleged historical necessity, a proof of being right and an excuse for being self-righteous. The triumph of Prussia in the Napoleonic wars and the efficiency and rationality of Prussian administration (which was then probably the best in existence) constituted for Hegel the proof that Prussia represented the triumphant march of history. A century later, Lenin's victory in 1917, amid the chaotic Russian political scene, proved to Marxist historians the indubitable superiority of communism over the less successful political forms of socialism or liberalism. However, in point of fact, Prussia's temporary success—there is no longer any Prussia today, a situation which hardly anyone would have predicted in 1830 or 1880—was not due to any historical "necessity" but rather to contingent circumstances, as was the bolshevization of the Russian empire. Indeed, world history is not predictable by dialectical logic, nor is it in itself a world court of justice. On the contrary, it is the task of the thoughtful observer to judge the process of historical success from the point of view of its long-range practicality and the ethos of the means used, and then to view it and its circumstances in its historical perspective. I was always impressed by Lucanus' report of Cato's words *"Victrix causa diis placuit, sed victa Catoni"*—"The victorious cause pleased the gods, but the defeated cause pleased Cato." Even the gods apparently have often changed their minds in history, and what was heralded as the victorious cause has become sooner or later (often to the surprise of those involved) the cause of the vanquished.

I do not mean to deny the grandeur of Hegel's metaphysical conception of history nor to detract from Marx's lasting moral contribution, particularly his emphasis on the importance of economics and on the imperative of social justice as a fundamental condition for the dignity and welfare of man and society. To these two post-Kantian giants of German thought, we remain as indebted as we are to the Hebrew prophets or to Plato and Aristotle. Elements of their thinking will inextricably remain part of the Western mind. But as heirs of the Enlightenment we cannot return to a "new" Middle Ages of religious or secular dogmatism concerning the course of history and the salvation of man. We have learned to understand, better than the Enlightenment did, the infinite complexity of human nature and history, the inherent limitations of all human knowledge, the uncertainty of the human condition, and the necessarily subjective role that the historian (who must

be a conscientious scholar but cannot be a "scientist")
plays in the selection and evaluation of the voluminous
facts which the growth of research in the last century has
put at his disposal.

History easily casts its spell over man. There is hardly
anything more fascinating than the study of the past. At
least, for my generation, and for those generations immediately preceding mine, the study of history—a study
tremendously enhanced in depth of time by archaeological
discoveries, in breadth of space by the opening-up of new
lands, and in quantitative scope by the systematic discovery and intensified use of original sources—has held
the same fascination as astronomy did for the men of the
seventeenth and eighteenth centuries. Both subjects have
opened new vistas and given man a new self-understanding
and a new feeling of importance. Perhaps we shall soon
reach a point of diminishing return in the study of history
and, with the development of new spatial communications,
astronomy will recover its former pre-eminence. But the
fascination of history will continue because of the in-
vocative power of the dedicated historian, whose task may
be compared to that of the poet. Both make the past and
the present meaningful, and thus satisfy a basic need of the
human mind, essential at least to modern Western civilization, the need to render order to man's life and to understand its meaning.

The historian's power to fascinate and to evoke meaning can corrupt, like any other form of power. Unlike his
counterparts in astronomy and the sciences, the historian
must deal with the often conflicting interests of parochial
human groups. Thus it is not surprising that the interpretation of history often strengthens and extols national claims
and finds good reasons to place them above universal

ethical considerations. Ethical considerations more easily influence and restrain individual actions than group actions. In an individual, egoism, disinterest in one's fellow man or one's neighbors, is generally regarded as reprehensible. A similar egoism on the part of groups, in our time especially national groups, ceases to be reprehensible. On the contrary, it is glorified and sanctified as dedication to a greater "whole"; indeed, it becomes a *sacro egoismo,* dedication to the state through which the individual is believed to achieve his true self-fulfillment. Among nationalities, neighboring peoples are no longer regarded as "neighbors" in the sense of the biblical prescription. Among nationalities one's actions toward a neighbor—and these actions are performed with a clear conscience and, indeed, often with righteous pride—are the very kind of conduct which an individual would be least likely to display to a neighbor.

History easily supplies the justification for such an attitude. It disregards the categorical imperative of universality, of just treatment of one's fellow men, and substitutes instead the self-serving "exceptional circumstances" that allegedly justify the actions of one's own group. History was once the handmaiden of theology; for the last one hundred years it has been in danger of becoming the handmaiden of national or class interests and of providing absolution for all kinds of crimes which the individual conscience would not easily bear. There is no sure remedy against this danger. The historian can protect himself only by critical self-awareness of his inevitable bias, by as wide a circumference of human sympathy as possible (here the influence of the ancient Stoics should be gratefully acknowledged) and by broadening his own horizon through the comparative method of studying and presenting history. Though this is often difficult to do, when he views events in any nation, or the actions of a particular group in a given period against the background of universal history, it enables him to compare the claims and behavior of similar groups and nations in other periods, in order to gain perspective and objectivity in dealing with the specific movements and events he is studying. Such a comparative method will also enable the historian to become more fully aware of the dynamics of social and political change. The British historian Arnold J. Toynbee has provided us with a contemporary example of such a universal, comparative approach in his *Study of History*.

History is an open process; the unexpected and unforeseen may happen at any time. There have been instances of such dynamic historical change in my own lifetime, in fact, perhaps more in my lifetime than in other periods of history. I wish to mention here only two such recent examples since the end of World War II. The first is the existence in our postwar world of a new Austrian Republic and of a new Germany, a development hardly expected by anyone in 1930.

The West German Federal Republic, with its democratic constitution, is now oriented toward the West and no longer centered, as Germany was after the fateful wars of 1866 and 1870, on Berlin and the Prussian tradition. Its predecessor, National Socialist Germany, though in no way an inevitable outcome of German history (or, as most Germans thought only twenty-five years ago, its highest culmination), had deep roots grounded in German attitudes which originated in the "war of liberation" against Napoleon. These attitudes became widespread after Bismarck's triumph, and dominated German thought in the decades before World War I. We owe to the research of a

German historian, Professor Fritz Fischer of the University of Hamburg, a monumental work, *Griff nach der Weltmacht* (*Reaching Out for World Power*), on Germany's war aims and bellicose foreign policy before and up to the very end of World War I. The atmosphere of Wilhelminian Germany, which Professor Fischer's documentation reveals, explains the weaknesses of the Weimar Republic, which were manifested in the rise of extreme nationalist and paramilitary organizations, and, above all, in the election of aged Field Marshal Paul von Hindenburg, the symbol of imperial military glory and the spirit of World War I, as President of the Second German Reich —and this at a time of growing economic prosperity and when elections were still entirely free and democratic.

By contrast, in the West German Federal Republic established in 1949 there has been fortunately no official emphasis on the restoration of the Reich; there have been no secret subversive societies, no resistance movements, no Prussian militarist spirit, no large anti-Western political parties, which so many who remembered the fate of the Weimar Reich had feared would plague the growth of an orderly constitutional development in Germany. The election of a World War II general as Federal President was unthinkable in 1949. Germany in the 1920's had been a focus of nationalist and anti-Western unrest and a threat to the peace of Europe. Conditions are different in the Germany of the 1960's—the Germany of Ludwig Erhard's Christian Democrats and of a transformed and increasingly influential Social-Democratic party. This change in the moral and intellectual climate of Germany, which in 1930 or 1940 I would have thought impossible, certainly represents a surprising development, a new and unexpected turn.

Something similar has happened in Austria. At the end of World War I, after the collapse of the Habsburg monarchy, Austria became a republic. This First Austrian Republic, which lasted from 1918 to 1938, was the scene of a relentless and bitter struggle—in reality, a civil war— between Catholic Conservatives and Social Democrats, a struggle that led directly to the downfall of the Republic. Most Austrians, unhappy in their small land, longed for "union" with their "fellow Germans" in the German Reich. This wish was fulfilled when Hitler invaded and annexed Austria in 1938. Jubilantly greeted, the *Anschluss* was followed shortly by the disastrous chaos of World War II, into which the German Reich led a not unwilling Austria. But the Second Austrian Republic which emerged in 1945 after the disintegration of the Great German Reich had learned a sobering lesson. It has since been accepted by most Austrians as their homeland, and has shown a surprising stability and prosperity, based upon the willingness of the two once implacable and antagonistic parties to compromise and to cooperate.

A second unexpected and unpredicted development of our time is of even greater importance. Before World War II, it was generally assumed, and not only by Marxists, that imperialism was the basis of capitalist prosperity. This view was popularized by John A. Hobson's study, *Imperialism* (1902), and by Lenin's *Imperialism: The Latest Stage in the Development of Capitalism* (1917). It was regarded as inevitable that nations "hemmed in" by a lack of space or by overpopulation would seek to conquer and exploit colonies in order to create national wealth and support a rising industrial living standard. Capitalism, it was maintained, could base its prosperity only on the exploitation of backward peoples. Thus the thrust of imperialism, alleged to be the outcome of economic necessity, was depicted as leading inevitably to wars among the capitalist states—as if wars had not existed throughout history, long before capitalism. The real fact was that Marx, a keen observer of the European scene, but in many ways a prisoner of his own insights, universalized beliefs and observations that were valid only for his own "bourgeois" age and culture, a period in which economic developments loomed larger than in any preceding period of history and in which the attendant materialism came to full flowering. The slogan of the hour in mid-nineteenth-century Europe might well have been *"enrichissez-vous, Messieurs,"* yet this "get-rich-quick" philosophy would have been incomprehensible as a guide for life in thirteenth-century Europe or in Indian or African society.

After World War II, however, to the surprise of many, this typical nineteenth-century bourgeois emphasis on size and expansive strength, which Marx shared, proved wrong. The loss of their empires did not render Japan, Italy, France, or the Netherlands less prosperous. On the contrary, capitalism, divested of imperialism, did not lead to a growing impoverishment of the masses but to an unexpected and widely shared prosperity, greater than any known in history. The British Empire was at no time territorially more powerful than after World War I, yet a large segment of the population lived in economic misery. Not until the liquidation of their empire in the years after 1945 did the British people enjoy a higher standard of nutrition, health, and education than ever before.

Germany, after World War II, lost not only all of its colonies but much of the former territory of its homeland. And this truncated West Germany had to accommodate in its reduced borders about nine million refugees from East Germany. Yet the Federal Republic, by the early 1950's, had become more prosperous than the Wilhelminian Reich had ever been. At the same time, Germany was divided into a "capitalist" and a "Communist" state, a division that allowed comparison of the efficiency of the two systems. The populations of each state of course shared a similar heritage—they had the same educational and cultural background, the same disciplined habits and dedication to work. Most of the German industrial capacity is in the West, but even taking into account this factor, one has only to compare the economic condition of the two Germanies today to see how erroneous many of Marx's assumptions about capitalism were. Or, to speak with the caution which should characterize the historian, the widely held expectation of the 1930's that capitalism would collapse appears unjustified in the 1960's.

All this of course I neither saw nor understood before World War I. But what had become clear to me by then was the fact that most men are not guided primarily by rational or economic considerations, by aspirations of economic betterment or by enlightened self-interest, but by collective passions and emotions which silence rational considerations and efforts to be objective and to view differences from the other fellow's point of view. Objectivity demands not only cool heads but empathy, a willingness and intellectual ability to put oneself in the other fellow's place. Nationalists rarely display such an ability; they are all too easily convinced of the righteousness of their cause, and thus can see no merit in the cause of their "adversary." In my youth, in the atmosphere of Prague, with its pervasive mood of nationalist stirrings and historical romanticism, I myself succumbed to the fascination of such attitudes. I do not regret it, for later it gave me the opportunity to understand the nascent national movements in Asia and Africa and to become aware of them as early as the end of World War I. It allowed me to compare them with nationalism in Europe and to see their positive sides, which, however, are often endangered and turned into the negative when nationalist movements realize their goals by oppressing or displacing other peoples, or when they are based on aggression and conquest. The more I understood the fundamental character of power as the central drive in modern political life, the more I distrusted its glorification.

As a young man I was more impressed by Nietzsche than by Marx in my understanding of human motives. The will to power seemed to me stronger than economic considerations, self-centered nationalism with its power urge more representative of the times than a class-conscious concern for the equality of workers of other nationalities. The fact that in 1914 the overwhelming majority of all socialist parties decided to support the nation-state power struggle and to abandon internationalism; the evolution of leading socialists like Józef Pilsudski and Benito Mussolini into extreme nationalists; the attitude of Zionist workers in Palestine toward their Arab fellow workers; and finally the triumph of nationalism within Marxian-Leninist communism itself—these and many similar facts bore witness to the strength of nationalism as the leading and decisive motivating force of our age.

Nietzsche regarded the will to power as the fundamental trait of all human life. This it certainly is not. Will to power is characteristic of certain cultures and historical situations, and especially of the age of nationalism and imperialism, Nietzsche's own age, the nineteenth century.

Like Marx, Nietzsche was a representative of his time. But Nietzsche was not a nationalist; his will to power was an individual phenomenon, more characteristic of the pre-nationalist era of the Renaissance, or of a Napoleon (in many ways, the last Renaissance figure), whom Nietzsche revered. Nationalism represents the will to power as a collective phenomenon. Perhaps such a collective will to power was also present in Hellenic Greece, but neither Buddhism nor early Christianity knew this exaltation of power. Today, however, the nations of the West have spread this doctrine throughout the world. Rabindranath Tagore protested against it; but the Republic of India has succumbed to it. Will to power is no longer the prerogative of strong, exceptional individuals; it has become universalized and characterizes whole peoples. In our own age, the masses are often more driven by this will to power than are their governments or statesmen.

IV

MY EDUCATION

I GREW UP in what today would be termed a sheltered home atmosphere. My parents were good people. I never felt any hostility toward them, nor any strangeness or dislike. True, I did not feel especially close to them; I was not on intimate terms with them, nor was I given to express openly my affection for them. But I had no hesitation or difficulty in following the biblical command to honor one's father and mother, and I did not need the incentive which the Bible adds, which seems to me to detract from the moral value of the command itself.

My parents knew little of modern pedagogy or psychology but they had good common sense and cared deeply for the well-being of their four children, of whom I was the oldest. We were never poor, but when I was in my teens we often lived in quite modest circumstances. My father was a businessman, but he had no great business capacity; he did not plan carefully enough, and he was too trustful, and so was often taken in by relatives and friends. Later, when he abandoned his independent business ventures, which always seemed to start quite well but did not prosper, and became a salesman, he fared better and made a satisfactory though modest living. People felt attracted by his affability, his sense of humor, his

31

friendly manner of conversation. Like many salesmen, he liked to be with people and felt happier when on his travels than at home. He was a man of simple tastes, always neatly dressed. His only indulgence was that, like most Bohemians of his day, he liked to eat well. He was a good-looking man, whose appearance even in old age had something of the military. Until his mid-seventies, he enjoyed good health and continued his travels across Bohemia. He was familiar with its railways, the wooden-benched third-class carriages, and the modest provincial hotels. He was proud of his economic independence and of being able to provide for his children. He died while on one of his business trips, stricken in a railroad station, quite suddenly and without any prior warning of illness, in his seventh-sixth year.

My mother was probably the more intelligent parent, but of a less happy disposition. She came from a wealthier family and had received a more thorough education. As was customary in the 1880's, she went to a private finishing school for girls. She had learned French, and I owe it to her that during my childhood, as long as we could afford it, we had a mademoiselle living with us, a young woman from Neuchâtel, one of the French-speaking cantons of Switzerland, who taught us to speak French. Thanks to the "bourgeois" ambitions of my mother, I was later able to lecture in French, and for many decades I preferred French novels and poetry to the literature of other languages. From my own experience I am very much in favor of children growing up bilingual, or if possible even trilingual. It widens their cultural horizon and makes them more proficient in the nuances of their own language. I am certainly grateful that a knowledge of Latin and French was a part of my upbringing.

In her younger years, my mother played the piano rather well and read poetry avidly. She copied the poems she liked in a poetry album, which is still in my possession. I did the same thing for many years, though our tastes were naturally very different. She grew up during a period when taste in poetry throughout the Western world was at a low level, whereas I was fortunate to share in the great poetical and artistic rebirth of the turn of the century. When my mother grew older, which means when I knew her, she ceased playing the piano or reading poetry. As with so many other middle-class women of the period, the exertions of daily life took their toll. It is regrettable that the conventions of the time prevented my mother from going into business or taking up a career. She would have been more successful than my father.

In many ways, middle-class housewives then had an easier life than young middle-class women have today in the United States. There was always a servant in the family, and we were fortunate to have had in Marie Vrbová, called Mařenka, a dedicated cook and maid of all purposes, who came to my parents when they were married in 1890 and stayed with us for over forty years, until after my father's death. She must have been very pretty in her youth, for traces of beauty could be seen in her round Slavic face even in old age. But with the years she had grown stout and was burdened by overwork. Though illiterate, she was highly intelligent and was an expert shopper. In my life since I have found many "educated" persons much less intelligent and far less ethical than Marie. She taught me not to overestimate the effects of literacy. Partly thanks to her I know that illiterate Africans and Arabs may be wiser and better persons than those European university graduates who regard such backward peoples as "uncivilized." This, of course, does not mean that illiteracy is good, much less that it is a cure for the ills of this world. The "noble savage" naturalism of a Rousseau or a Tolstoy has always seemed naïve to me. The uncivilized person can be as savage as the educated man. How savage the educated man can be, my generation has witnessed since 1914.

At present there are no Mařenkas around. Their disappearance is also a sign of the total transformation of society within the lifetime of my generation. But today's young women—particularly in the United States—are much better trained to assume responsibilities than they were in Europe in my mother's generation. I have taught young women in America for many years, and when I later meet them as housewives and mothers, I am always much impressed with how well they handle their various tasks without servants, how they often are able to hold down professional jobs at the same time, and above all, how they find time to participate so actively in cultural and social work. This, of course, reflects the great progress in the American woman's education and her acceptance of her role in life. Fortunately, since World War II many European countries have been following the example of the United States in this respect. In Europe, too, men are beginning to marry much younger and to count much less on a dowry than they did in my father's time.

Within the narrow limits set by the custom of the time, my mother took excellent care of her home and children. Her marriage was in all probability an arranged affair, as was then usual on the Continent. She brought my father an appreciable dowry, again in accordance with European custom. Though the marriage was not happy— a situation caused in part by differences of temperament and worsening financial circumstances—it was an average marriage, as good as many born of romantic love. My mother was twenty-five, my father ten years older, when they were married in October, 1890. Eleven months later I was born.

Both my parents were of Jewish families who had lived for generations in the Czech countryside. Both were bilingual, though the language used in their families' homes was predominantly German. My mother, Berta Fischer, was born in Kralupy, a small town about twelve miles north of Prague on the Moldau River, where her father owned a brewery. I never knew her parents; they had died long before I was born. My father, Salomon E. Kohn, outlived my mother by eleven years. My father's parents were still living, in the small village of Nová Cerekve, when I was born. They reached a ripe old age, as did all of their children, and though I never really knew them—I was brought to visit them once when I was nine months old—I remember photographs showing them as typical patriarchal figures.

Of my great-grandparents I know nothing. They are lost among the many Jewish generations who since the tenth century have peopled Bohemia, suffering all the humiliations and persecutions to which Jews, like other religious minorities or underprivileged classes, were subjected in Europe until the period of the Enlightenment, which began the process of political and social emancipation and integration of all oppressed creeds and castes, a process still going on today and gaining rapidly in scope and spread.

I have never had much interest in attempting to trace my own ancestors. The living generations and their future have been my concern. Nationalism, which was in its initial stages a forward-looking movement of emancipation stressing individual dignity and liberty, later (particularly in Central and Eastern Europe) came to stress the past, to emphasize the "blood" or the race, as if this "blood" were a peculiar life force that could determine the conduct and thought of present generations. Ancestry, and especially one's parental home, certainly is one of the elements influencing a person's character and life, but it is only one of many elements. Sometimes it can mean very little, as everyone knows who has reflected on the disparity in children born to the same couple or on the great differences and lack of understanding between generations.

The granting of full legal equality for Austrian Jews, in the Constitution of 1867, plus the rapid growth of urban centers in the latter half of the century, resulted in a large-scale migration of Jews from small country towns and villages to Prague and other cities. German became or remained the main language of these people. It was the language of the administration, it was also the language of a great culture; an education in Czech did not offer either of these advantages. Only with the growth of the Czech national movement and of a modern Czech culture did a growing number of Bohemian Jews regard themselves as Czechs and prefer to speak Czech. In 1921, after the establishment of the Czechoslovak Republic, there were, according to official statistics, about 80,000 persons of the Jewish faith in Bohemia, just over 1 per cent of the total population. Of these, 37,000 regarded themselves as Czechs, 26,000 as Germans, and 10,000 as of Jewish nationality.

The Prague Jewish community was not rich, but many Jews were well-to-do, and extreme poverty was rare. Only very few Prague Jews were members of the Orthodox faith. My father went to the synagogue only on the high holidays, my mother almost never. None of the ceremonial laws were observed in our home. Yiddish, the language of the majority of Eastern European Jews (many of whom lived in distant and to us little-known provinces of the monarchy), was not spoken in Prague. In fact, until World War I, which brought to Bohemia many refugees from Galicia, there was little contact between the Bohemian and Yiddish-speaking Jews; the Eastern European Jews were regarded more as aliens than as "brothers." Even the Central European Zionists before 1914 did not learn Yiddish, the language of the people; if they learned anything they learned Hebrew, which because of its biblical substance seemed the nobler language.

Yet the Prague Jewish community could look back upon a great past. My earlier reflections about the spirit of history being so alive in the monuments and streets of my native city also held true, though to a lesser degree, of its Jewish past. By 1910, however, evidence of this past had almost disappeared, both in the outward character of the city and in the consciousness of its inhabitants. Until the 1840's, Jews were obliged to live in a separate community, with its own special laws and subject to special, severe restrictions. In 1852, this ghetto was incorporated into the city as one of the five administrative boroughs, and its name was changed from *Judenstadt* (Jews' Town) to *Josefstadt,* in memory of Joseph II. Around the turn of the century an urban renewal project replaced the narrow, dark, teeming lanes of the ghetto with new and wider streets flanked by the modern apartment houses of that period. What had become in the latter part of the nineteenth century a romantic, mysterious haunt of poverty, prostitution, and crime in which less than one-fifth of the population were Jewish, now became a middle-class residential district, where many Jewish families returned to live.

Despite this new urban development in Josefstadt at the turn of the century, some remarkable architectural monuments of the past were preserved. Characteristically, they belonged to the two great periods of Prague's history, the Gothic and the Baroque. The *Altneuschul,* Prague's oldest synagogue, was originally built in the eleventh century. (Since the Middle Ages, German- and Yiddish-speaking Jews have called their meetinghouse of prayer and learning *schul,* a word derived from the Latin *schola,* and used by Luther to translate the Greek New Testament term *synagōgē.*) Its main parts, including the beautiful entry door, are typically fourteenth-century Gothic, as is its dark and gloomy interior. In its center stands the *almemar,* the platform where the Torah, the Pentateuch, was read to the congregation; there hangs the gold-embroidered flag donated by the Emperor to Prague's Jews for their defense of the Charles Bridge against the Swedes during the Thirty Years' War. According to legend, the *Altneuschul* was built by refugees forced to leave Jerusalem after the destruction of the Temple by the Romans, constructed of stones of the Temple; and at the coming of the Messiah, it is said, the stones will be flown back to Jerusalem to rebuild the Temple there.

From the same period date the ancient tombstones in the old Jewish cemetery, which served as a burial ground until the end of the eighteenth century. Lilac trees grew there and bathed the narrow, winding paths with their fragrance every spring. The most ornate stone covers the tomb of the great Rabbi Löw Judah ben Bezalel, who died in 1609 and who was equally famous as a miracle worker. Legends attribute to him the creation, in clay, of an artificial man, the Golem, the prototype of Mary Shelley's *Frankenstein* and Karel Čapek's *R.U.R.* Next to the cemetery stands the Baroque Jewish Town Hall, with its Hebrew clock.

At the beginning of the twentieth century, however, little of the Jewish tradition lived on in Prague. None of the Jewish children among my acquaintances knew Hebrew or Yiddish or had anything more than the most superficial knowledge of Jewish history or religious literature. The official and compulsory religious education in the public schools, given by rabbis, did little to foster Jewish tradition or sustain its deeper religious sentiments.

From the emancipation on, which at the time of my birth was hardly a quarter of a century old, Prague's Jews played an important role in the cultural life of the city, especially among the German population. At the end of the eighteenth century, Prague University had granted the first doctorates in medicine and in law to Bohemian Jews. By 1900 there was a large number of Jewish lawyers and physicians, writers, and students in Prague, though most Jews continued to belong to the merchant class.

As is typical of Jewish parents, with their high respect for learning, most of the merchants, even those of the poorer class, wished their sons to receive the best possible education and to become university graduates. So, my parents sent me to a private school maintained by the Piarist Fathers. The members of this order, the *patres scholarum piarum,* in addition to their three regular vows, obliged themselves to teach without remuneration. At that time they were especially active in Austria and Poland. Their elementary school in Prague, in the Herrengasse (the street on which Rainer Maria Rilke was born), was mostly frequented by Jewish children. As far as I know, no attempt was ever made by the Fathers to influence or convert their pupils, who received a more thorough and vigorous training there than they would have in the public schools. Father Anton Hesky, who taught me the entire five years I spent there, was a strict disciplinarian. Thanks to him I acquired an excellent background in grammar and spelling and maintained the position of "primus" (first in the class) throughout my subsequent eight years of secondary school. While I was in secondary school I visited Father Hesky every year to report on my progress and plans. I was much too young to form an opinion about the value of the Piarists in general, but I have preserved for many years grateful memories of my teachers and of the quiet, severe, and awe-inspiring interior of the school building. Now it has long receded into the past. The First World War, as far as I know, ended the activities of the Piarists in Prague.

The same fate overtook the public classical high school, the Altstädter Gymnasium, which I entered in 1902, a year after Franz Kafka had been graduated from there. It occupied much of the second floor of the vast eighteenth-century Kinsky Palace. The beautiful Baroque front of the building faced the Old Town Square, the Altstädter Ring, one of the loveliest and most imposing squares to be found anywhere. There stands the ancient Town Hall and opposite it the Gothic Tyn Church, the center of the Hussite movement. The north side of the square is occupied by many quaint houses of various periods, and the south side opens onto a view of the green slopes of the Letna hill across the Moldau. On the ground floor of the Kinsky Palace, Kafka's father at that time operated a textile store.

I spent eight years in the Altstädter Gymnasium, from

my eleventh through my nineteenth year. These years
seemed then very long to me, and the passage from the
lowest grade (the Prima) to the highest (the Octava)
appeared very slow. (Since then, as is often the case as
one gets older, a progressive acceleration seems to have
occurred in the rhythm of my life.) My teachers, though
not brilliant, were on the whole competent men. All of
them had received the degree of Doctor of Philosophy and
were minor scholars in their own right who had written
their dissertations and were expected to produce learned
articles periodically for the annual reports of the Gymnasium. Some of them I still remember; the kindly Wenzel
Rosicky, who taught mathematics; the rather learned
Joseph Wihan, who taught German, knew English and
Italian well, and had published some studies in comparative literature; the pompous Hugo Ostermann, who taught
history and was a good lecturer, but who, like most history
teachers in Central Europe, overstressed nationalism and
patriotism in a fashion that we today would associate with
Fourth of July orators in the United States. The director,
or principal, of the Gymnasium, Anton Frank, impressed
us by his personal dignity and the enthusiasm with which
he taught and recited Greek. Our "ordinarius" in the
Obergymnasium which comprised the last four years was
Karl Wolf, a quiet, handsome man, who taught Latin.
Most of the teachers lived in very modest circumstances.
Their personal lives were unknown to us, but we did know
that Wolf played first violin in a quartet which met in his
home. Occasionally he invited some of his students to
these affairs. I still remember the formal, somewhat stuffy
décor of his home. At a time when the phonograph and
the art of recording were in their infancy, such quartets
were common. Though technically they may have lacked

a great deal, they added charm and a note of festivity to home life.

I do not share the negative attitude sometimes voiced concerning the curriculum and methods of the pre-World War I Austrian Gymnasium. True, my generation did not receive, as students in Oxford still did in 1910, a classical education in its pure form. Translations from German into Greek and Latin and the writing of Latin verses had been abandoned before my time. But we still had eight years of Latin—the first two years on an eight-hours-a-week basis, all the following years for six hours a week—and for six years we took five hours a week of Greek. The only modern language offered, besides Czech, was French, and this was on an elective basis. No one thought then of Russian, not even in the Czech schools. I knew enough French so that I did not need to take it in school; further-more, my French was greatly helped by my knowledge of Latin, an indispensable foundation for the Romance lan-guages and English. Even today I can hardly imagine a mastery of modern European literatures or languages with-out some knowledge of their Latin and Greek bases.

World War I ended this kind of training, as it did the systematic memorization of poems in the classical and modern languages. In my own generation, the practice had considerably lessened, but as a youth I met many older people—lawyers, physicians, officials—who could recite from memory, and with unrestrained enthusiasm, long pas-sages from Homer or Horace.

My study at the Gymnasium ended in a final, compre-hensive examination, called a test of maturity, correspond-ing to the French *baccalauréat* and entitling the successful candidate to enter the University. I passed it at the top of my class. Today, apart from history, I probably would fail most of the subjects which I then had more or less mastered—calculus and plane trigonometry, certainly Greek, and probably Latin. But that is true not only of what I learned in school. *"Non vitae, sed scholae discimus"* ("We learn not for life, but for the school"), Seneca wrote, reproachfully. That is true throughout life, for to forget—and that means to change—is part of life. And yet something lives on, be it only a faint memory. This death of knowledge is a universal phenomenon and does not concern only the so-called "dead" languages (as if a language immortalized in great literature and in the memory of generations could ever die). How much "living" knowledge and skills I have learned and unlearned again in the course of my life! As a youth I played the piano—I studied it with the blind writer Oscar Baum, a friend of Max Brod and Franz Kafka—and I learned to read scores. I used to sit in the top gallery of the Prague Theatre on the dimly-lit steps leading to the standing-room enclosures and follow *Meistersinger* or *Tristan* from the scores without looking at the stage. I could not do it today, but I enjoyed it then and learned from it. I carried many of these scores with me on all my many later migrations and only very recently gave them to a young musician who can now put them to better use.

When I lived in Siberia I learned to speak Russian fluently, and in Palestine I lectured in Hebrew. My fluency in both languages has grown a little rusty since then, but they stood me in good stead when I needed them. Even today I still read much in Russian.

As a youth, I learned, or tried to learn, dancing and fencing from old-fashioned masters, and I played tennis and skated. As a high school student and even in my army days, I played chess, checkers, and occasionally cards, and

enjoyed it. Since 1917, all this has receded into a faraway
background. After World War I, when, it seemed to me,
the whole world suddenly became addicted to sports,
dance-crazy, and mechanically minded, I did not. I never
danced or drank after 1914, I never learned to swim or to
ski, to drive a car or to use a typewriter, not out of principle but because this was not my style of life. Few men
can do justice to many things—Goethe was one of the ex-
ceptions—and I had to put aside what seemed to me the
nonessentials, partly out of inertia and partly out of
natural inclination. Could I start again anew, I might do
many things differently—who would not?—but I believe I
would not do so in order to conform to the trend of the
time.

But change has consequences even beyond the mere for-
getting of much of what one has learned or known. One's
circle of friends and acquaintances is also always shifting
and re-forming. I have met so many people, gotten to know
them well, even intimately, and then had them drop out of
my life. Perhaps I would have learned and unlearned
much less and had a more circumscribed knowledge and
group of friends if I had lived my whole life in Prague, as
I expected to in 1914.

The problem of continuity and change is one of the
fundamental problems both of history and of individual
life. How different I am from the young man who entered
the German University in Prague in 1910. How greatly
changed is the Union of Soviet Socialist Republics today
from the Russian Empire of the Romanovs, indeed, from
Stalin's Russia. How different is the United States of today
from the United States of Herbert Hoover to which I
came in 1931. Yet in all this change there is continuity:

the two are basic and interconnected processes. Their proportion varies according to circumstances. But without change there is no history, no life, no development. For that reason no living entity, a man or a people, can ever be fully defined.

The same is true of an individual's own likeness. I look at photographs of myself as a child, a teen-ager, a young man, even as a man in his forties, and I hardly recognize myself. Is this me? There are resemblances, of course, but there are also great differences. Often, when I see a man or woman whom I have known in days long past, it is fascinating to try to rediscover somewhere beneath the changes imposed by time some of the traits which call to mind long-forgotten sentiments. From time to time we all seek to recapture the past, to embark upon *la recherche du temps perdu* ("the quest of bygone times")—though no time truly lived is ever really bygone and lost. It lives on, sometimes with such a strength that we must beware against becoming its prisoner.

This transitory element of all life sometimes frightens and confuses us. A great Viennese poet, whom I read with loving admiration in my youth, Hugo von Hofmannsthal, has expressed the melancholy wisdom of old age in verses written in his youth in his "Terzinen über Vergänglichkeit" ("Terza Rima on Transitoriness"):

> Dies ist ein Ding, das keiner voll aussinnt,
> Und viel zu grauenvoll, als dass man klage:
> Dass alles gleitet und vorüberrinnt.
>
> Und dass mein eignes Ich, durch nichts gehemmt,
> Herüberglitt aus einem kleinen Kind
> Mir wie ein Hund unheimlich stumm und fremd.

This is a thing which no one can fully comprehend,
A thing too monstrous to be bewailed,
That everything in life flows on and passes.

And that my very self, unimpeded,
Has passed across the years from a small child
Uncannily mute and alien to me.

V

ZIONISM

In the summer of 1908, when I was seventeen years old, I became a Zionist. As far as I remember I made this decision quite suddenly, without much soul-searching. I was about to enter the Septima, the penultimate class, in the Gymnasium at the time. And so for the last two years there and during my four years at the University, I was a zealous member of the association of Jewish university students which called itself Bar Kochba. Bar Kochba was the Jewish military commander who led the last revolt (132-135 A.D.) against the Roman domination of Judea. Bar Kochba claimed to be the Messiah, and was so recognized even by Rabbi Akiba, one of the greatest scholars of that age. After initial successes, the revolt was crushed when the fortress of Bethar on the Mediterranean, south of Caesarea, was captured.

Although the name of the association recalled the warrior-like nature of the messianic nationalist movement, the Bar Kochba in Prague was something different. In my time, the Bar Kochba association opposed the military spirit and the messianic expectations that its name suggested. It was a small group of very serious-minded young men, deeply concerned with cultural values and ethical

duties. Since I have long led quite a different kind of life
from that of most of my companions of that time, I may
be allowed to say that it was intellectually and morally as
outstanding a group of young men as I have met. Among
them I wish to mention only two.

Hugo Bergmann, a classmate of Franz Kafka in the Altstädter Gymnasium, was of strict Jewish background and
was one of the very few Zionists outside Eastern Europe
who mastered the Hebrew language and migrated to Palestine—he settled there immediately after World War I—
without being forced to do so by anti-Jewish feelings or
threats. He soon became a deeply religious Jew and later
a professor of philosophy at Hebrew University. During
my later stay in Palestine, the two of us edited, in the
spirit of the pre-1914 Bar Kochba, two Hebrew books.
One book was dedicated to the memory of the German
anarchist-socialist Gustav Landauer, killed in Munich in
1919. The other book was dedicated to Aron David Gordon, a Tolstoyan figure who at the age of fifty emigrated
from his native Russia to Palestine. There he became a
worker on the land and the spiritual father of the
"pioneer" movement. In the tradition of Tolstoy but also
of the Hebrew prophets, Gordon did not believe in state
power, politics, or diplomacy but espoused instead the
ethical action of the individual. A people cannot be
"redeemed," Gordon taught, by political success, even less
by military victory, but only by the spiritual and moral
rebirth of its individuals. He coined the Hebrew term
am-adam, the human people, which we used as the title
of our book, and by which he meant a people guided
solely by ethical commands in its relations with other
peoples, as the individual man should be in his relations
with his fellow men. Gordon went to great lengths in

opposing the formation of a Jewish legion to "reconquer" Palestine for the Jewish people in World War I. He died in 1922 in Daganiah, the first *Kwutsah,* or communal settlement, which he helped found in 1908 at the southern end of the Lake of Tiberias.

To return to Bergmann: In 1919, before he settled in Palestine, he published a collection of German essays, now long forgotten and out of print, under the title *Yavne and Jerusalem,* which perhaps best reflects the spirit of the Bar Kochba to which I belonged. Yavne was the place where Yokhanan ben Sakkai, a pupil of Hillel, took refuge when the Romans besieged Jerusalem in the year 70 A.D. In the spirit of the prophets, he espoused the cause of peace with the Romans, was friendly to them as he was to all, and opposed the zealots who fought for the country's independence and wished to defend Jerusalem to the very last. He escaped from besieged Jerusalem into the Roman camp and asked to be allowed to make Yavne a spiritual center. The Jewish state perished in the war. The Jewish community, however, was able to live on because of the foundations that Yokhanan laid in Yavne, which made possible the survival of the Jewish people and assured its intellectual and spiritual creativity.

My other close acquaintance in the Bar Kochba was Robert Weltsch, who was born in the same year as I but was one year ahead of me in the Altstädter Gymnasium and at the University. He was chairman of the Bar Kochba for the academic year 1911-12, and I succeeded him as chairman the following year. Together, during my chairmanship, we edited the symposium *Vom Judentum (On Judaism),* in which, among others, Martin Buber, Karl Wolfskehl, and Gustav Landauer coöperated. Weltsch and I became very close friends in the last years of the Gym-

nasium, and in spite of the different paths our lives have
since followed, we have remained very close friends for
well over half a century. He later became the leading
Zionist editor, perhaps best compared with Walter Lipp-
man in American journalism. After World War I he lived
in Berlin for twenty years, then for seven years in Palestine. Since 1945, he has resided in London. Although we
have never lived in the same city after 1915, we have
visited frequently, save for the war years, and we have corresponded with great regularity, often more than once a
week. We both learned shorthand at the Gymnasium,
where it was taught as an elective course, primarily as an
aid in taking notes. We have put it to good use in our
correspondence. The system which we learned, invented
by Franz Gabelsberger (1789-1849), is no longer taught;
we are probably among its last surviving practitioners.

A close and intimate friendship of over half a century
which outlasts long separations and the vagaries of fate is
indeed a rare and wonderful thing. Our thinking has often
been identical, not only on historical events but also about
men and daily affairs. We hardly needed to talk; a hint
was enough for mutual understanding.

In 1927, Weltsch and I published a book in German
called *Zionistische Politik*, long since out of print. It was
a collection of essays dealing with problems of Zionism.
Weltsch's essays dealt with the central political problem of
Zionism, the relationship with the Arabs. Before 1914, the
political realities of Palestine, and political problems in
general, interested us little. This, as I shall point out,
changed after World War I. In 1919, when I was in Irkutsk, Siberia, I published an article in the local Zionist
paper *Yevreyskaya Zhizn* (*Jewish Life*) in which I stressed
that Palestine's Arabs, who formed 90 per cent of the

population, were then, like all Asian peoples, under the sway of an incipient but strong nationalism; they were convinced that Palestine was their country and that they should exercise their right of national self-determination. Weltsch shared my belief in the fundamental importance of the Arab problem. In an essay written in 1925, he pointed out that Palestine could prosper only if a relationship of mutual confidence were established between the two peoples. "Such a relationship can only be established if those who are the newcomers—and such we are—arrive with the honest and sincere determination to live together with the other people on the basis of mutual respect and full consideration of all their human and national rights."

Weltsch added that he did not then find such a determination among most Zionists. On the contrary, he noted a lack of tact and an unconcealed chauvinism, an attitude which he rejected not only for ethical but also for realistic reasons. "The realization of Zionism is unthinkable," he wrote, "if we do not succeed in integrating it into the ever-stronger nationalist awakening of the neighboring Asian peoples. The public opinion of the world cannot forget the existence of a large native population in Palestine; the growing sympathy with the aspirations toward national self-determination of native peoples will make Zionism unpopular in many circles, not out of antipathy with its essence nor out of anti-Judaism but out of consideration for the natural rights of the Arabs."

The article aroused a storm of indignation among many Zionists in 1925. And even among the few who were then inclined toward Weltsch's point of view, some changed their minds after 1933. Hitlerism was a traumatic experience, and under its influence many Jews concluded that Hitlerism was not an isolated phenomenon, only possible

in the German setting of its time, but an indication that
the Enlightenment, with its hopes of emancipation, had
failed, and that the implacable hostility of the non-Jewish
world toward the Jews was a permanent phenomenon.

The extreme nationalism that prevailed in Central and
Eastern Europe at that time, and the triumph of fascism
in so many European countries, seemed to confirm the end
of liberal democracy and humanitarian ethics. In 1933,
the year of catastrophe for the Germans, the Jews, and
the whole world, Weltsch, as editor of the official Zionist
organ in Germany, took a rational and courageous stand
against the growing German madness. This stand won
him the approval of the Zionists, and in 1935, when his
paper celebrated its fortieth anniversary, he was applauded
by many who once had violently opposed his position on
the Arab question. As a reply Weltsch reprinted his article
of 1925 and stressed that he was prouder of that article
than anything else he had written: "In the third year of
National Socialist rule, if we do not—of our own initiative,
without being forced to do it—integrate the rights of the
Arabs into our conception of a future Palestine, if we do
not reject clearly and resolutely the boycott which some
Zionists proclaim and practice against the Palestine Arabs,
then we shall lose the right to speak for the Jews in the
Diaspora in the hour of distress. For we regard nothing
as more abominable than a policy [of double standard]
based upon a double-entry bookkeeping. It is our hope . . .
that we do not prove right those who regarded the Jewish
ethos only as a means, born out of the situation of a weak
minority, [and alleged] that given different external conditions, the heathen will-to-power would prevail among us,
too. For then Zionism would, in our opinion, lose its soul."

I quote these sentences because they express so well the

character of the Zionism we believed in before and immediately after World War I. Later developments seemed
to prove us wrong, at least temporarily. Zionist nationalism
went the way of most Central and Eastern European
nationalisms. But whatever the present or the future was
to hold, my participation, for almost twenty years, in the
Zionist movement enriched my life in many ways. It gave
me a better understanding of the pitfalls and self-decep-
tions inherent in most national movements and political
activities. Its most positive result was to direct me to
study the Bible and the modern works of scholarship about
ancient Jewish history. I learned Hebrew, and later, as a
prisoner of war in Siberia, I read and translated, together
with my friend Hugo Knoepfmacher, modern Hebrew literary works into German.

This new Hebrew literature which developed after 1890
was part of the modern literary renaissance among all
European peoples of that time. I noted with interest the
strong influence of Nietzsche and of the then fashionable
paganism and hedonism of European literature on this
new Hebrew literature. Equally important for my intellectual growth were my personal contacts in this period.
I was privileged to meet in the Zionist movement a number
of interesting, attractive, complex personalities, many of
Russian origin, representing the best traits of the old Russian intelligentsia. They are all dead now, as is the period
which they represented.

It was a Hebrew writer from Russia, Asher Ginsberg
(1856-1927) writing under the pen name Ahad Ha-am
("one of the people"), who exercised a great influence
upon my thought at that time. Born into a very orthodox
Jewish family, he was not exposed to modern European
and Russian civilization and languages until early man-

hood. He was less influenced by the apocalyptic and revolutionary visions of the Russian intelligentsia of the turn of the century than by the rational, evolutionary approach of English philosophy. His Zionism was not centered, like Herzl's, around the political oppression and the poverty of the Jewish masses or on the existence of anti-Semitism; rather, it was an attempt to continue the prophetic heritage of Judaism in a creative spirit. A Jewish state or majority in Palestine seemed to him not only impracticable (as far back as 1891 he drew attention to the importance of the presence of the Arabs in Palestine, a fact often overlooked by Zionists) but also inessential. He wished to create a "spiritual center" on a sound economic basis, whose truly Jewish life would radiate from Palestine and regenerate Jewish life in the Diaspora. For that purpose Jews were to come to Palestine not driven by necessity and persecution but spontaneously, out of a spiritual rebirth.

Jewishness meant to Ahad Ha-am the ideas of absolute justice and above all of impartial objectivity, relying on the spirit and not on the sword. Therefore the Jewish community in Palestine could not resemble other national movements. On November 18, 1913, in a letter to one of the Jewish pioneers in Palestine, Ahad Ha-am protested against the boycott which the Zionist labor movement had proclaimed against the employment of Arab labor: "Apart from the political danger, I cannot put up with the idea that our brethren are morally capable of behaving in such a way to men of another people. Unwittingly the thought comes to my mind: If it is so now, what will be our relation to the others if in truth we shall achieve 'at the end of time' power in Eretz Israel [Palestine]? If this be the 'Messiah,' I do not wish to see his coming."

Under the influence of Ahad Ha-am, we were cultural rather than political Zionists. This corresponded to my general attitude, which made me doubt the wisdom of augmenting the number of nation-states and proud sovereignties, and to my distrust of reliance on numbers and power. But it should be pointed out that the leader of political Zionism, Theodor Herzl (an immensely attractive personality, according to those who knew him), sketched in his last novel, *Altneuland,* a vision of the future which was not essentially very different in its conception from Ahad Ha-am's insistence on the ethical relationship of the Jewish people to its neighbors. In that novel, which he regarded as the legacy he left to his movement, Herzl did not envisage a Jewish state, but a New Society, in which the Arabs prospered and multiplied, as did the Jews. Herzl castigated self-centered nationalism and anti-Arab sentiments and attitudes as a negation of his aspirations. I believe today, as I did then, that only such a vision of a New Society can bring about a fulfillment of Zionism in the Middle East, and I hold fast to the prophetic tradition of Judaism which Ahad Ha-am rightly stressed.

VI

INTELLECTUAL ROOTS

A̲ₗₜₕₒᵤ₉ₕ ALTHOUGH I DID NOT fully realize it at the time, European culture was entering an era of rich and exciting development in art, literature, poetry, and music that was to have a profound and lasting influence. Around the turn of the century, there was a veritable cultural renaissance in Europe. It was a time of excitement and high expectations. A new poetry and a new sensibility to form were reflected in the works of Stefan George, Hugo von Hofmannsthal, and Rainer Maria Rilke. A new music, whose foremost representative was Gustav Mahler, spread from Central Europe. From France came the first news of an art which made the Impressionists seem old-fashioned—Cézanne, the Fauves, Braque, and Picasso. A new humanism was in the air, and we breathed it eagerly. Politics and social sciences, by contrast, seemed minor matters.

I was not enrolled in the humanities faculty at the University but rather the faculty of law and political science, *Rechts- und Staatswissenschaften*. At that time, in Austrian universities, political science and theory, political economy, and international law formed part of the curriculum of the Law School. I still consider this a sensible arrangement. Political scientists thus know the law thoroughly, and lawyers are familiar with political economy. Law students had to take two semesters of philosophy, and the law itself was taught with an emphasis on its historical foundations, so that the future lawyer became acquainted with the rich details of Roman law and its development, canonical law, and the history of old German law. To a certain extent, the study of law in Austrian universities played the same role as did classical training at Oxford and Cambridge. In both cases this training served as the traditional preparation for entry into the higher civil service positions as well as to the "gentlemanly" occupations in which one could still pursue his general cultural and intellectual interests.

In my years at the University I had no clear idea where the study of law would lead me. My chief interests were philosophy, literature, and theology. The only lectures I regularly attended throughout the years were those of Anton Marty, the senior professor of philosophy at the University. He "read"—and this word fits, because he did not lecture but recited from an old creased, handwritten manuscript, full of additions and alterations—his comments every day at noon. Though he was a poor lecturer, he was the only one of my University professors who made an indelible impression on me, not because of the philosophy he expounded (which I soon abandoned) but because of his personality.

Marty was a Swiss Catholic from the canton of Schwyz who had taken holy orders but had left the Church, as had his teacher, Franz Brentano, to whom he remained devoted throughout a lifelong friendship. Marty and Marty's disciple, Oskar Kraus, who succeeded him in the Prague chair, were the "most faithful of the faithful" among the many thinkers influenced by Brentano, of whom the best known were Alexius Meinong and Edmund Husserl (who dedicated his first book, *Philosophie der Arithmetik* [1891], to Brentano). Brentano was perhaps less influential through his writings than he was as a Socratic teacher. The same may be said of Marty. Though his life and personality lacked the brilliance of Brentano's, there emanated from this delicate, quiet man, who seemed afraid of even the slightest bit of wind or fresh air, a great moral and intellectual strength. I was to have the good fortune to encounter such strength again in men like Leonhard Ragaz, the Swiss Protestant theologian and socialist, and Joshua Radler-Feldmann, the Zionist pioneer and orthodox Jew who lived for almost half a century in Palestine and wrote under the pen name Reb Binyomin.

I knew Franz Brentano only through the descriptions and comments of his disciples, but he must have been a powerful personality. He came from an intellectually and artistically most distinguished German family. Ordained as a Catholic priest, he later left the Church and taught in Würzburg and Vienna, and then settled in 1896 in Florence. He and Marty found their masters in Aristotle, in the Scholastics, in Leibnitz, Locke, and Hume—in what might be called "sober" philosophy; they criticized Kant for his "Copernican revolution," according to which man's cognition is not determined by things but things by man's cognition. They rejected all post-Kantian idealism (Fichte, Hegel, and Schelling) and all forms of mysticism. The true method of philosophy, for them, was that of the natural sciences—*"Vera philosophiae methodus nulla alia nisi scientiae naturalis est* ("The true philosophy has no other method than that of natural science"), Brentano said in his disputation when he was called to teach philosophy in

Würzburg in 1866. Brentano and Marty regarded a descriptive, empirical psychology as the foundation of philosophy.

Though Brentano did not belong to any religious faith, the certainty of God was for him beyond doubt. Like his brother Lujo, who taught political economy at the University of Munich, Brentano was a liberal who wished to restrict the activities of the state and leave citizens the largest possible scope to pursue their own lives as they chose. He opposed militarism, recognized one, and only one, ethical norm, which was the same for the individual and for the state, and he abhorred the principle of "my country, right or wrong."

I will always remember the sunny summer morning in 1914 when I saw Marty for the last time. He was then a dying man, even more delicate than he had been. He spent the summer, as we did, in Schelesen, a village typical of the serene, beautiful countryside. I walked slowly at his side in the garden amid its radiant stillness and peace. War had been declared. Like most of my generation, I was willing to take this event in my stride, probably because we had no glimmering of its reality or of its awesome consequences. The air was heavy with patriotism and heroics. In his thin, wavering voice the old man remarked that war was the greatest misfortune that could befall mankind. I never forgot his words nor the deep sadness of his voice.

Brentano and Marty disagreed with Kant's epistemology, but their views on the state and the individual, on peace and war were not so far from Kant's. When Brentano died early in 1917 in Zurich, no clergyman officiated at his grave; only Friedrich Wilhelm Foerster, the German pacifist, spoke a few words. In the same year, Oskar

Kraus published the first German translation of Jeremy
Bentham's little-known *Principles of International Law,*
written seven years before Kant's famous pamphlet *On
Perpetual Peace.* Marty's lectures I have forgotten; his
books, dealing mostly with the structure and philosophy of
language, I never read. But his personality and his role
as dedicated friend of wisdom unswayed by political passions live with me.

Among the writers whose work influenced me, though
their approaches were very different, were Kant (both the
ethical and political writings), Schopenhauer, Nietzsche,
and Bergson. Schopenhauer and Nietzsche were especially
heady wine, at once a temptation and an inspiration. The
same was true of Bergson, who wrote as well as they did
and had much in common with them. But I did not reread
much of Schopenhauer or Bergson after the 1920's. They
belong to my youth.

My experiences with Kant and Nietzsche were different.
As I grew older, I gained a new and deeper understanding of both; first, Kant, later, Nietzsche. Kant's sober enthusiasm for individual liberty and for the moral forces,
represented for him in the Enlightenment and in the
French Revolution, his categorical imperative that no
utilitarian consideration could justify a deviation from the
moral law and that every human being must be treated not
as a means for one's own progress but as an object of
infinite worth, seemed to me in accord with Nietzsche's
fundamental belief in free self-determination, though out-
wardly they seemed to conflict with Nietzsche's concept of
a moral elite. It may seem strange to link Kant, the model
small-town scholar, who led a life of exemplary regularity, and Niezsche, the homeless wanderer, who was at
bottom an artist but thought of himself as a prophet. But

both were rigorously ethical beings who cared deeply for the independence and dignity of the individual, and both were daring intellectual revolutionaries. Nietzsche was also one of that small band of nineteenth-century nonconformists whose ranks included Ralph Waldo Emerson and Henrik Ibsen. Though the ways in which they presented their cases and lived their lives were very different, I have come more and more to see their similarities. They were the opposite of the modern "organization man," a term not yet coined then but a reality well known to Emerson and Ibsen.

In the years before 1914, German intellectuals rediscovered romanticism and mysticism. Schopenhauer, Nietzsche, and Bergson were "romantic" philosophers, philosophers of the life force, of the Will, of the mysteries of vitality and struggle, and of artistic creativity. To use the term introduced by Nietzsche, the balance and moderation of the Apollonian gave way to the Dionysian yearnings and strivings for the infinite, to passion and the passionate, to the quest of the unknown, to the search for new experiences and sensations. This was often expressed in the image of a "return" to nature, to ancestors, something soul-stirring and profound, primeval and primordial, which the Germans labeled *Urgrund*. The mythos of the *Urgrund* (the German prefix *ur-* is untranslatable into other languages but implies something abysmally profound, original, and peculiarly valuable) had a great impact on German writing of the period. It aroused a new *frisson,* a thrill of excitement that consecrated enthusiastic but unclear thought and longing.

The romantic poets and thinkers at the beginning of the nineteenth century—Hölderlin, Novalis, Friedrich Schlegel, and Adam Müller—who long had been neglected

and were almost unknown around 1900, were rediscovered
and re-edited. The German youth movement of that time
emphasized the free and independent individual. Simultaneously, the young were agitated by the longing for a new
and vital human community, the *Gemeinschaft*. This
"organic" community was contrasted with the cold, artificial, and purely legal or utilitarian society, the *bürgerliche
Gesellschaft,* of the Western, particularly the English-
speaking, world. German youth longed for a new leader, a
trusted and beloved charismatic authority, instead of the
established authorities of state, school, and paternal home.
They spoke less of "organization" than of "movement."
The spirit of restlessness, an intellectual and moral *Wan-
derlust,* took hold of a generation which seemed eager
to plunge into the unknown to reach new shores. There
was a great deal of vague, verbose talk about *Aufbruch,*
an awakening and departure to new horizons and new
destinies. It went hand in hand with an exaggerated self-
esteem, and was an impassioned appeal to heroism, to the
spirit of sacrifice, to a rejection of the comfortable bourgeois life.

Much in this new attitude came directly or indirectly
from Nietzsche, but it also led to a fascination with the
past, with roots, with the "folk," with the preconscious,
and with nationalism, which Nietzsche rejected and which
he fought so bitterly in his last years. German intellectuals
spurned the rationalism of the Enlightenment as superficial and "Western," as alien to German heredity. They
found this heredity buried deep in the preconscious of the
German race, in folk traditions, in blood and the soil. The
most varied influences combined in the decade before
1914 to direct our thought into these channels. Reason

was believed to be insufficient to penetrate to the deeper
levels of human experience.

Ethnography and anthropology also began to supply
new avenues to probe the darker layers of the mind. The
first volume of Sir James Frazer's *The Golden Bough, A
Study in Magic and Religion* appeared in 1907. *"Dans
tout esprit humain, quel qu'en soit le développement intel-
lectuel, subsiste un fond indéracinable de mentalité primitive"* ("In every human mind, whatever its intellectual
development, there survives an ineradicable foundation of
primitive mentality"), wrote Lucien Lévy-Bruhl. The once
undisputed authority of classical Greek art as the culmination and model of all art was shaken by the discovery
and appreciation of Egyptian and Oriental art, and soon of
primitive African sculpture. The Viennese school, which
included not only Freud but writers like Arthur Schnitzler,
explored the subconscious and threw new light on the
mysteries of dreams, childhood, neurosis, and sex. The
German publishing house of Eugen Diederichs in Jena
began to publish a translation of the works of a little-
known Danish theologian, Sören Kierkegaard. The same
publisher offered to the German reader the works of Bergson, books on German and other mythologies, on Oriental
wisdom, and on the "soul" of Russia. In the quest for
new understanding, many Germans turned from the West
to the East and to Russia.

Diederichs also published modern editions of the great
German mystics, from Johannes Eckhart and his disciples
Heinrich Suso and Johann Tauler, to Jakob Boehme, who
stressed life's mysterious realities which can only be experienced, not described in the manner of the rationalism
of theology. In 1914 I intended to edit a selection from the
German mystics and I began to negotiate such a project

with the well-known publishing house of Langewiesche. Nothing came of it, but the article which I contributed to the symposium *Vom Judentum* was called characteristically "Der Geist des Orients" ("The Spirit of the East"). The thoughts and sentiments that moved us so deeply have since been reiterated many times—the desire for a richer, more meaningful life, as opposed to the fragmentation and futility of "modern" existence, and the need for realizing one's true self by endowing existence with a deeper meaning and a sense of purpose. How this was to be achieved, we were as unable to say as are those who today complain about mass culture and alleged lowering of intellectual and cultural life.

Our reading at the University was highly eclectic. It ranged from the post-Kantian philosopher Johann Gottfried Fichte, and his heavy-handed rhetoric, to the poetic of Chuang-tzu, the Chinese Taoist philosopher to whom we were introduced in Buber's German edition of his works published in 1910 by the Insel Verlag, and then in 1912 in Richard Wilhelm's translation published by Diederichs. Our own writing style was more influenced by Fichte than by Chuang-tzu. Fichte interpreted the *I* as the ethical will, and the world as the material in which the will should create that which ought to be. We transferred Fichte's lectures on "The Vocation of Man" and on "The Characteristics of the Present Age" into the context of our own situation, and we accepted his appeal to bring forth the ideal community by placing all the power of the rationally and ethically mature individual at the service of his own nation.

In his *Reden an die deutsche Nation* (*Addresses to the German Nation*), which after long having been forgotten had then become fashionable among German youth, Fichte proclaimed the German mission to realize the ideal national community. He thought the German people were called to this task because subjection to foreign rule and assimilation of alien ways had brought as its fruit the deepest level of misery—he spoke at the time of Napoleon's occupation of Berlin—and yet, as no other people, the Germans had managed somehow to preserve their integrity as a people. A new national pride and sense of destiny could not fail to arouse in them the awareness of their true self and of their vocation that would enable them, by a moral and spiritual regeneration, to reassert their own freedom and that of Europe as a whole. To us, the lesson was clear. The Jews of our time seemed to find themselves in a position similar to that of the Germans on the eve of the rise of their nationalism.

Martin Buber was the man who brought us the new German thought and widened our intellectual horizon. In January, 1909, he delivered before the Bar Kochba the first of his *Reden über das Judentum* (*Addresses on Judaism*). For the next five years our student organization provided the platform from which Buber's work exercised a strong influence on the youth of Central Europe. He made us keenly aware of the vocation of man and the vocation of Judaism, and he showed us this vocation as a new life. Nineteenth-century Jewish scholarship, in conformity with the thinking of the time, had interpreted Judaism as a rational religion and had paid little attention to its mystical undercurrents or its subtle primitive myths and legends. In keeping with the new trend—the word "mythos" became very fashionable in early-twentieth-century Germany —Buber revealed the existence, outside "official" Judaism, of a subterranean Judaism and its manifestation in the pietistic-mystical sect of Hassidism, which had flowered in the eighteenth century among Eastern European Jews. For us and for the German reader, Buber retold the Hassidic sayings and legends in a language, itself much influenced by the taste of the period, which moved our hearts and enriched our minds.

Later, after the First World War, Buber changed his style, and in the place of the *unio mystica* with God he put the encounter of man's *I* with the great *Thou*. He turned from mysticism to a religious existentialism and became one of the leaders of contemporary thought. Lately, his importance has been recognized in the English-speaking countries, where he was still unknown until just before the Second World War. (The first English translation of one of his works appeared only in 1937—*I and Thou;* however, from 1945 to 1960 no less than twenty of his books appeared in English translation.) Before World War I, the time I am now discussing, he not only published his first Hassidic books and his *Addresses on Judaism* but he gathered and edited the ecstatic confessions, myths, and sagas of many peoples, from Ireland to China.

How strongly Buber was influenced—and we, in turn, by him—by the German thought and style of the period may be shown by referring to a sentence from his introduction to the *Kalevala,* the national epic of the Finns, which he edited in 1914. He characterized this epic, in his almost untranslatable Germanic style, as *"von des Volkes Urträumen geboren, im breiten Leben der Volkszeiten erwachsen"* ("born out of the *ur*-dreams of the folk and matured in the broad life of folk history"). Buber referred to Elias Lönrot, the modernizer of the Finnish national epic, in these terms: *"aus Blut and Schicksal der tragenden, wesenerhaltenden Volksschichten gekommen"* ("one who had come out of the blood and destiny of those folk-circles who represented and preserved the folk spirit"). Blood, destiny, and the organic folk-community then played a great part in nationalist German thought, and these fateful words, opposed to the spirit of the age of the Enlightenment, shaped our thought, too. However, we transferred their significance from German to Jewish nationalism.

In those days before 1914, Buber was a young man, in his early thirties, hardly ten years older than we were. We, rightly, looked up to him. His moral earnestness, his capacity for hard and concentrated work, his broad scholarship, and his brilliant insights in so many varied fields of human culture made him the leader of a youth eager for deeper spiritual experiences. Like Ahad Ha-am, Buber did not base his Zionism on persecution or economic exploitation, nor did we. We knew little of either. Anti-Jewish persecution had little to do with our Zionism. True, the Czechs on the whole were unfriendly to the Jews, and many of the German students who came to the Prague University from the Sudetenland were racists and pan-Germans. But in the Austria of Francis Joseph we felt secure, and our own largely German Jewish circle in Prague offered us a sheltered existence. Our Zionism was not a reaction to persecution but, under the influence of the German thought of the period, a search for "roots," a turning inward toward the supposed center of our true self, which dated back, so we believed, over two thousand years to biblical times. Some Zionists wished to revive the spirit of the conquerors of Canaan under Joshua ben Nun, others that of the Hebrew prophets. From this latter point of view we gained a new, positive relationship to early Christianity. We, of course, did not accept Jesus as the

Christ but we honored him as one of the greatest Hebrew prophets, a religious ethical anarchist, to whom the powers and ambitions of the age meant little compared with the approaching *malkut shomayim*, the Kingdom of Heaven, whose coming he announced to the Jews and which would put an end to the injustices on this earth.

The implications of this emphasis on blood and ancestral heritage as the determining force of human life were not fully clear to me at that time. Some of my friends went so far as to believe that a man of Jewish ancestry and cultural heritage could never become or be a true German, Italian, Frenchman, or Dutchman. He could never be fully integrated into the life of any "host" nation; he was and must remain an alien everywhere except on his own "ancestral" soil, by which we meant not the soil of his grandparents or great-grandparents, but that of his ancestors, real or imaginary, of fifty generations past. Richard Wagner and other German intellectuals had said the same thing a half-century earlier. Of course, such a belief in biological determinism ran counter to the spirit of the Enlightenment, but my young friends proudly rejected the heritage of the Age of Reason.

Such, then, were our views as we lived our lives as students in prewar Prague; soon the experience of the Great War would change my whole outlook, and I would turn away from the ideas then current in Central Europe and rediscover the heritage of the Enlightenment.

VII

INTELLECTUAL LIFE BEFORE 1914

B︎UBER'S INTELLECTUAL breadth preserved our Zionism from cultural narrowness and made our nationalism compatible with a broad humanitarian and cosmopolitan outlook. At the same time, official nationalism throughout Central Europe was characterized by a narrow, militant patriotism which regarded the destiny and power of the nation-state as the most important premise of political life and as the spiritual fulfillment of the individual's own life.

We owed it to Gustav Landauer, Buber's friend, that our nationalism was tempered by an emphasis on mankind. Landauer was a "utopian" socialist who was influenced by Joseph Proudhon and who rejected the determinism and emphasis on class struggle in Karl Marx. Landauer stressed the human, ethical, and spiritual values in socialism. He was a pacifist, and he condemned the use of force by socialists as well as by capitalists. He was neither an economist nor a social scientist but a humanist. He edited the works of the fourteenth-century mystic Johannes Eckhart, and published two volumes of studies on Shakespeare.

Thinking about Landauer, I am inclined to compare him with Albert Camus, though Landauer never exercised a comparable influence and was not as creative a writer. Landauer can also be compared with the great French socialist leader Jean Jaurès. He was like Camus and Jaurès in his generosity, his knowledge of the complexity of the human condition, his deep concern with man. Like Jaurès, Landauer pointed out long before 1914 the danger of a great European war, but he did not believe that the socialist parties would be able to stop the war machine. Ironically, Jaurès was killed on the eve of the war by a French nationalist fanatic; Landauer was murdered by German nationalist soldiers in Munich at the very end of the war.

In the cultural field, as students at Charles University, we participated fully in the German and European life of the period. As typical Europeans, we paid little attention to English or American literature. For reasons I cannot remember, I took private English lessons for several years with a Mr. Lus who had emigrated in his youth to the United States, had become a citizen, and then had returned to Prague to open a language school. However, my study of the English language and of English literature —I remember particularly reading Dickens, for whom I could never develop much enthusiasm—did not give me much insight or understanding of British or American culture and traditions. American history, civilization, and literature were not taught in European universities, as far as I know, certainly not in Prague. Poe and Mark Twain were widely read in translations, but not really understood in all their complexity; Melville was unknown; Ralph Waldo Emerson was regarded as a minor Thomas Carlyle. The only American writer who appealed to us was

Walt Whitman, but for special reasons which I shall soon discuss.

But though we were on the whole unfamiliar with, and little interested in, American and English literature, we knew the writers and poets of Germany, France, Russia, and Scandinavia rather well. Prague itself had just produced a number of important German writers, including Rainer Maria Rilke and Paul Leppin, Franz Kafka and Max Brod, Franz Werfel and Johannes Urzidil. In spite of the small German population, there was a "Prague school" of German literature during this period. As *The Times Literary Supplement* wrote in retrospect half a century later, "In 1912 German literature embraced an almost embarrassing wealth and diversity of talent."

I was an avid reader and collector of German poetry in those days, and Rilke was my favorite poet. I knew many of his poems by heart and used to recite them with enthusiasm to my girl friends. Of the German classics, Hölderlin inspired me most at the time, whereas Goethe, not only his poetry, but his marvelous life and wisdom, opened themselves to me only in later years. Among French writers, partly thanks to the influence of Max Brod, Flaubert's *Éducation sentimentale* and the poems of Jules Laforgue interested me the most. My later life in France, after the war, gave me the opportunity of broadening my tastes to embrace much of modern French literature, from Stendhal, Baudelaire, and Rimbaud to the writers who dominated the literary scene around 1920.

Fortunately for me, many German publishers at the beginning of the century were bringing out the works of the major contemporary Russian and Scandinavian writers in excellent translations. Though I had never visited Scandinavia (I was to make two brief visits at a much later date), I became an avid reader of a number of Scandinavian authors, some little known to this day in America —Jens Peter Jacobsen, Henrik Pontoppidan, Herman Bang, and Karl Gjellerup among the Danes; Ibsen, Björnson, Jonas Lie, and Knut Hamsun among Norwegian authors; but only Strindberg and Selma Lagerlöf of the Swedish writers. The emergence of Scandinavian literature as a full partner among the older European literatures was almost of equal significance as the simultaneous flowering of Russian literature.

In the field of the novel, I preferred—and still do today—non-German authors. But in poetry, my heart belonged to those writing in German. And truly, in my youth, German poetry was more exciting than it had been at any period since Goethe and Hölderlin. This was perhaps also true of the theater, but I did not take as keen an interest in playwrights, with the exception of Ibsen, whom I regard as the greatest, and perhaps the only enduring, dramatist of modern times. Ibsen's real impact in Europe came through performances of his works in German. This was the era of both the classical theater cultivated in the Vienna *Burgtheater* and the experimental theater in Berlin (in which the stage manager or producer was equally important with, or more important than, the poet and the actor). But I found that I was more deeply moved by a poem read aloud several times in the stillness of my room than by the festive atmosphere of great theatrical performances, though I also enjoyed their drama and visual impact.

The years of my early manhood (1908-1914) coincided with the birth of the Expressionist movement in German literature, a movement closely allied with a similar trend in painting and sculpture. Expressionism was a very complex and even contradictory movement of small, disparate groups, in some ways a forerunner of surrealism. It was a reflection of the deep ferment in the intellectual and moral atmosphere of Central Europe on the eve of the First World War. The Expressionist movement produced a few great poets and painters and some interesting playwrights and short-story writers. Many of these men have since disappeared from the scene, leaving their brief testaments on the pages of equally short-lived periodicals that were once so eagerly awaited by their few but devoted readers. Today, they are rare finds in libraries and in catalogues of secondhand bookdealers.

These periodicals bore characteristic titles like *Der Sturm, Die Aktion, Das Neue Pathos, Pan,* and *Die Argonauten.* The publishing house of Kurt Wolff in Leipzig, where my symposium *Vom Judentum* appeared in 1913, was for the new movement what Diederichs was for neoromanticism and publishers like S. Fischer and Die Insel for the older literary generation. From 1913 to 1921 Kurt Wolff published a series of pamphlets containing poems or short stories, called *Der Jüngste Tag (The Youngest Day,* or *The Day of Judgment),* which expressed the two aspects common to all the Expressionist writers—their youth and their apocalyptic vision. When the eighty-sixth and last pamphlet appeared in 1921, the movement had already begun to peter out. Doomsday had apparently come and gone without changing mankind. Their youth had either perished or was growing old.

Expressionism was a protest against the period's conventionality, a search for a new reality and new forms. Its style was explosive, exclamatory, dynamically overstated, and ecstatically vague. Like Nietzsche and Dostoevsky, the Expressionists lived with the apocalyptic vision of approaching catastrophe, and their reaction to it varied according to their personality. The examples of three great poets of the early Expressionist generation may help illustrate these contrasts.

George Heym grew up in Berlin and died in January, 1912, at the age of twenty-four. A few months before, he had written in his diary: "I suffocate with my enthusiasm in this time of banality. For I need immense outward emotion to be happy. In my fantasies I see myself always as a Danton, or a man of the barricades. I cannot think of myself without my Phrygian cap. I at least hoped for a war. . . . Living always in storms, as wild and chaotic as the world, unfortunately always in the need of a great enthusiastic public to be happy, sufficiently ill, to be ever dissatisfied with myself, I would become suddenly healthy, a God, redeemed, if I could hear somewhere a tocsin, if I saw men running, their faces torn with anxiety, if the people rose up. . . ."

Georg Trakl was born in the same year (1887) as Heym, but spent his youth in Salzburg, Vienna, and Innsbruck. In August, 1914, he was sent as a medical soldier to the Galician front. Unable to live amidst the horrors of war, he committed suicide three months later. There was nothing of Heym's violence in Trakl's sensitive, tormented soul, which like his work was overshadowed by a deep melancholy.

Different was Franz Werfel, who was born in Prague one year before I was. His emotional pathos did not suffer from the pessimistic lashing out or the dark despair of Heym or Trakl. In his youth, Werfel had much in common with Walt Whitman. He sang of a humanitarian humanism, the hope of the universal brotherhood of all human beings, the promise of a harmonious life for all

mankind. He exalted in his confidence in man, his deep
love for, and sympathy with, all men—above all with the
poor, anonymous masses who live out their lives in great
cities and all those whose lot it was to suffer in life (an
influence of Baudelaire found in most Expressionists).

The first volume of Werfel's poems, *Der Weltfreund*
(*The Lover of Mankind*), appeared in 1911. It was filled
with recollections of his childhood in Prague. It also contained a comforting message of hope for all men, particularly for young men; it stressed the fellowship of all human
beings, not in the abstract sense of "mankind," but in
terms of real people no matter how diverse their lot in
life.

Werfel's second book of poems (1913), *Wir Sind* (*We
Are,* or *We Exist*), placed an equal emphasis on the community of the We and on the miracle of Being and Life.
When Kurt Pinthus edited his 1919 anthology of Expressionist poetry *Menschheitsdämmerung* (*The Dawn of Humanity*), he characteristically titled its four sections "Fall
and Cry," "Awakening of the Heart," "Summons and Revolt," and "Love Man," and he ended each section with
one of Werfel's poems.

After the war, Werfel married the widow of Gustav
Mahler, the remarkable Viennese woman who had been
intimately connected with Walter Gropius and Oskar Ko-
koschka. Like Friedrich Schlegel's wife, she was considerably older than her husband. Werfel wrote mostly novels
after his marriage. They were translated into many languages and made him well known abroad. But his novels
never communicated to me the excitement and exhilara-
tion of his early poems.

I have indicated that Whitman's democratic love of the
people found an echo in Werfel's youthful poetry. Werfel's

poem "To the Reader," the penultimate in his first book, is the very opposite of Baudelaire's famous *"Au Lecteur"* that introduces *The Flowers of Evil.* "My only wish, o man, is to be related to you," Werfel wrote. "My fellow man, when I sing of my recollections, do not be hard, melt with me into tears! For I have lived all lives . . . Thus I belong to you and to all! Please do not resist me! O, if it could happen once that, o brother, we fall into each other's arms!" A youthful voice here echoes Schiller's and Beethoven's sentiment in the "Ode to Joy." There was little of the apocalyptic mood and the stark melancholy of other Expressionists in Werfel. His was an ethical poetry: Salvation could come only from within man, not from institutions or political movements. This message coincided with what we had learned from Buber and Landauer.

Like Max Brod and other of Prague's German authors, Werfel introduced some of the great Czech poets of that day to the German public, in particular, Otakar Březina, whose free rhythms expressed a joyous, ecstatic optimism (influenced by Nietzsche after an earlier brush with Schopenhauer's pessimism) and Petr Bezruč, whose powerful evocation of the misery of Czech miners in Silesia was anything but optimistic.

In Prague, as in Vienna, the theater was popular to a degree found in few other cities. True, this public interest was less broadly based than its interest in soccer. (At the age of fourteen I myself began my writing career as a reporter for a Stuttgart sports weekly. My only payment was a free pass to the grounds of the Deutscher Fussball Club, the leading German soccer team.) Yet, except for the very young and underprivileged, the people of Prague followed events in the theater with a greater intensity than events in the sport world. Performances were the subject of heated discussions, and they were long remembered. Actors filled the role of today's TV and movie stars, though the public then was much less interested in their private lives than in their acting. (Sports and theater events alike were conducted along strictly segregated national lines. The Deutscher Fussball Club played leading teams from abroad, but it did not play Slavia or Sparta, two excellent Czech teams of that time, although their soccer fields were next to each other on the Letna hill.)

The Czechs are a theater-loving people, and the creation of a National Theater played a central role in the nineteenth-century nationalist movement. The National Theater was, of course, only one of the several Czech theaters in Prague. The Germans had, in my youth, two first-rate theaters. Like many Central European theaters, they offered a varied repertory of classical and modern plays and of operas, presenting different works each day. The smaller of the two theaters was the Theater of the Estates in the Old City, a late eighteenth-century rococo building. It was opened in 1783 with Lessing's tragedy *Emilia Galotti*. The most memorable day in its history was October 29, 1787, when *Don Giovanni* was given for the first time, with Mozart and the author of the libretto, Lorenzo da Ponte, present.

The Theater of the Estates was the older of the two German theaters and carried the inscription *"Patriae et Musis"* (in the eighteenth century "patria" meant not the nation-state—Czech or German—but the homeland of Bohemia, including all its ethnic groups). The second theater, the New German Theater, which opened in 1888 in the borough called the New City, had a different background. It was a consciously national creation. Today it seems astonishing to me that the relatively small German population in Prague could maintain a large repertory theater of this kind, with good drama and excellent opera. Its director from 1885 to 1910 was Angelo Neumann, one of the dedicated Jewish followers and apostles of Richard Wagner. (Wagner loathed Jews but accepted their services when he found them useful. Neumann's devoted efforts conquered many German stages for Wagner, who lived in ostentatious splendor and therefore welcomed the considerable increase in his income.) In 1876, Neumann produced *The Ring of the Nibelungen* in Leipzig, its first performance outside Bayreuth, and he opened his Prague career with the Ring cycle. (His son Karl Eugen was a scholar known for his excellent translations of Buddhist texts into German; I still have them in my library, forty years later.)

Neumann brought all the famous actors and singers of the day to the New German Theater. The yearly May festival of performances *(Festspiele),* since imitated in many cities, was a high point in our lives. Werfel's love for Verdi probably was developed there. My friend Robert Weltsch was a devoted opera fan, and he knew many of the operas, especially those of Verdi and Meyerbeer, by heart. My favorites at that time were Rossini's *The Barber of Seville* (which like all operas was performed in Prague in translation) and those of Wagner. Today, half a century later, I am still enthusiastic about Wagner (with the exception of *Parsifal,* which I first heard in Prague in 1913), but I have also come to love Mozart's *Don Giovanni* and *The Magic Flute* and Richard Strauss's *Der Rosenkavalier* and *Elektra.*

I am not certain whether cultural life holds as much excitement for young people today as it did for my generation. Perhaps they devote more time to serious study and to political life than we did, and this is probably a good thing. The chief difference between 1914 and 1963, it seems to me, is that we were under much less pressure to plan our future careers and to know what role we wanted to play in society than are young people today. As another point of comparison, my generation, even on the eve of World War I, gave little thought to the danger of war or its awesome consequences, whereas today few young people could afford such an attitude.

VIII

A TURNING POINT
IN WORLD HISTORY

THE SUMMER OF 1914 was one of the loveliest I have known, warm and sunny, promising not only a good harvest but a rich and bountiful life. However, fate and the irresponsible intransigence of government officials and military leaders decided otherwise. In the course of the following years I was to learn a lesson which I never forgot. This lesson was one as old as man, and it has been voiced repeatedly but never more clearly than by Axel Oxenstierna, the seventeenth-century Swedish chancellor, who is credited with having said, *"An nescis, mi fili, quantilla prudentia mundus regatur?"* ("Don't you know, my son, with how little wisdom the world is governed?")

Things have not improved noticeably since the days of Oxenstierna. There have been many decent and intelligent men among the "great" of this world, of course, but even they are all too often the victims of power and pride. In the wars I witnessed, none of the statesmen or generals involved demonstrated any prescience about the outcome of the conflict or its effects on the very causes for which it was fought. All of which is to say that war is an inade-

quate means for achieving the purposes which the leaders
of warring nations profess to pursue.

The calamity which was to change so many lives began
on Sunday, the 28th of June, 1914, a beautiful early summer's day. The people of Prague were out for a Sunday
stroll, on the boulevards and in the parks, or enjoying beer
and music in some charming outdoor restaurant. I was
sitting with a friend in the cool, quiet Café Radetzky, a
typical Austrian café in one of the oldest parts of Prague,
the Malá Strana, or Kleinseite, at the foot of the Hradčany. Both of us were in the midst of preparing for the bar
examination, which, as things turned out, neither of us
was to take. Around three o'clock the headwaiter, a tall,
erect old man in his seventies, laid before us, with trem-
bling hand, a special edition of the local daily. Its large
headlines tersely announced that the Archduke Francis
Ferdinand, heir to the Habsburg throne, had been assas-
sinated in Sarajevo, the capital of Bosnia. During the
Russo-Turkish War of 1878, Austria had occupied this
former Turkish province, which was inhabited by people
speaking Serbo-Croatian, a Southern Slav language. Serbia,
which had gained her full independence as a result of this
same war, now aspired to unite all Southern Slavs under
Serbian leadership. She only recently had taken another
major step toward this goal as a result of her victories
over Turkey and Bulgaria in the Balkan Wars of 1912-
1913. Bosnia itself had long been a hotbed of Serbian sub-
version and intrigue against Austrian rule. Now, on this
lovely Sunday in August, fanatical Serbian students had
committed murder in the name of nationalism—one of the
high-minded, self-righteous acts of brutality sanctified in
the name of country which were to be repeated so often
in the years to come.

Whatever his personal shortcomings, Francis Ferdinand was no tyrant. Nor was he without sympathy for Slavic aspirations. To protect Slavic interests, he wished to curtail the prerogatives of the Magyars, and he hoped to make the Southern Slavs equal partners in a federated monarchy. He was very happily married to a Czech countess (who was killed at his side) and had, for the sake of "the woman he loved," renounced his children's right to the succession. The old Emperor did not like him, and most Magyars and Germans were strongly opposed to his rather vague pro-Slav sympathies.

Despite the solemn headlines, people soon began to turn their thoughts to other matters. The summer weather continued glorious, and so we decided to go to Schelesen for the long summer vacation. Life there seemed peaceful and undisturbed, exactly as in previous years. The newspapers contained little news that seemed to give cause for concern, and besides we knew that Europe had been free of war (save for the chronic conflict in the Balkans) for nearly half a century. The diplomatic scene appeared normal. The German Emperor was on his yearly cruise in northern waters. But behind this deceptive façade, German and Austrian military and diplomatic circles were busy laying the groundwork for a course of action which would "settle" the Serbian problem once and for all. Confident of Germany's backing, Austria pursued its demands against Serbia at the risk of a general war. Exactly one month after the assassination at Sarajevo, Austria declared war on Serbia. One week later the war had become the Great European War. Today many think of it as the greatest war ever fought. For this war, which started in 1914, ended only in 1945. It radically changed the political and social order of Europe.

Perhaps World War I can best be compared to the Peloponnesian Wars, which ended Greek pre-eminence in the ancient world. The historian Thucydides considered the wars of 431-421 B.C. and of 414-404 B.C. a contest of two power systems neither of which could tolerate an appreciable gain of power in the other nor any diminution in its own power or prestige. Thucydides believed that the struggle between Athens and Sparta was "great and memorable above any previous war. For both states were then at the full height of their military power, and the rest of the Hellenes either siding or intending to side with one or the other of them." Thus any conflict, even a minor one, was bound to spread and to involve all Greece. The situation in Europe in 1914 was not fundamentally different.

Thucydides went on to say of the Peloponnesian Wars what could be said of the European war of 1914-1945: "No movement ever stirred Hellas more deeply than this; it was shared by many of the Barbarians, and might be said even to affect the world at large. . . . [It] was a protracted conflict, attended by calamities such as Hellas had never known within a like period of time. Never were so many cities captured and depopulated; and several of them were repeopled by strangers. Never were exile and slaughter more frequent, whether in the war or brought about by civil strife."

In 1914 no one foresaw that the war would become a protracted holocaust, a decisive turning point in world history. It is important to remember the mood of the public in 1914 and to note how entirely different it was from that of our own day. Then, in spite of a feverish armaments race and violent press campaigns, the public underestimated the possibility of war and had but little idea of the destructiveness of modern warfare.

Germany put its trust in its military superiority, and its fear of the loss of this superiority was an important factor in bringing about the war. Germany expected a quick, decisive victory, and so felt that it could afford to disregard the moral aspects of its conduct and the weight of an unfavorable international public opinion. The chiefs of the German and Austrian general staffs—Helmuth von Moltke and Conrad von Hötzendorf—believed that 1914 was the right moment, perhaps the last moment, for the Central Powers to gain an easy victory. Austria-Hungary was determined not to appear weak in the face of Slav aggression, whereas Russian nationalists were equally determined not to appear weak by not supporting their Slavic brothers.

Austria-Hungary's fundamental mistake lay in its past history—in the rejection of a federal constitution, in the compromise with the Magyars, in the alliance with Germany. The Habsburg monarchy's *raison d'être* was to promote peace in multiethnic Central Europe. To that end it should have followed a policy of neutrality, similar to that of Switzerland, satisfying the political needs of its peoples on a federal basis and pursuing neither a German nor Magyar, neither a Slav nor Latin, policy.

The Austrian occupation of Bosnia-Herzegovina in 1878 was a step in the wrong direction. Austria should have remained free of entanglements with Berlin and St. Petersburg; by doing so, it might have become a force for moderation that might have restrained those two aggressive, centralized military powers.

In his "Lectures on Modern History" delivered at the turn of the century, Lord Acton pointed out that in Berlin and St. Petersburg a type of government unfamiliar to the

West was being developed. "Government so understood is
the intellectual guide of the nation, the promoter of
wealth, the teacher of knowledge, the guardian of morality, the mainspring of the ascending movement of man."
And, indeed, this was the way in which the Russian and
the German governments saw their task, long before the
rise of totalitarianism in those countries. "That is the tre-
mendous power," Acton continued, "supported by millions
of bayonets, which grew up [in the eighteenth century] at
Petersburg, and was developed, by much abler minds [in
the nineteenth century] at Berlin; and it is the greatest
danger that remains to be encountered [by the English-
speaking peoples]."

Fortunately, no such government existed in 1914 under
the Habsburgs. But Austria-Hungary allowed itself to be
drawn into, indeed, willingly entered the twentieth-century
conflict between the Russian and German powers. And
that conflict destroyed Austria-Hungary and ended the era
of peace and stability the Habsburg Empire had helped
to assure to multiethnic Central Europe.

As I have said before, few if any of us at that time had
any idea of what the war might mean. We were convinced
that it would be a short war, probably over by Christmas,
1914, and that no modern state could survive the financial burden of a longer war. None of the peoples of Europe
was prepared for a long war. No one thought of it as a
war to end wars, nor, indeed, was it an ideological war at
the beginning (except to a few German professors, who
saw it as a fulfillment of Germany's *Kulturmission*).

Our approach was dictated by a traditional patriotism—
we were going to war in defense of our fatherland, which
we believed to be in danger. And in most nations, the
people were as eager as the government to protect their

nation's power position and prestige. National pride and
hatred of the adversary were found on all sides. We regarded the war as another of the many struggles we had
learned about in school, struggles which had been fought
by our fathers, grandfathers, and forebears throughout history. In 1914 many young men even welcomed the war,
viewing it as an exciting adventure. Individual military ex-
ploits, acts of bravery and heroism still exerted a powerful appeal to youthful imaginations. Few of us realized
how mechanized warfare would soon become. There still
seemed ample room for the deeds of daring we had learned
about in classrooms and in books.

My friend Robert Weltsch and I joined the same infantry regiment. It was a Prague regiment and therefore
mostly Czech. In August, 1914, the Austrian Germans
and the Magyars were as enthusiastic about the war as
were their German allies. The Czechs were much less enthusiastic. The Austro-Hungarian army was fighting as
Germany's ally against the Serbs and the Russians, both
of which were Slavs like the Czechs. The Czechs realized
that a German victory might well strengthen German and
Magyar control over the Slav peoples. In fact, the German
Chancellor, Bethmann Hollweg, appealed to racial loyal-
ties in characterizing the struggle as a conflict between
the Germans and the Slavs. Thus there was no enthusiasm
for the war in our regiment. On the other hand, army life
was not too oppressive; it consisted mainly of boredom
and of waiting for something to happen. Even in the army
the Austrian character remained relatively easygoing.
Then, in early October our regiment was transferred to
Salzburg—probably to isolate us from the "evil" influence
of Slavic Prague.

In 1914, the armies of Europe were the most visible

remnant of the feudal order. A special medieval code of honor and etiquette governed officers' attitudes. The gulf separating the officers from the rank and file was unbridgeable. Ordinary soldiers were transported to the front in cattle cars; in fact, these cattle cars carried the inscription "For forty men or six horses." However, soldiers with higher education were better treated. They could enter the officers' training school, as Robert Weltsch and I did in Salzburg.

The shift to Salzburg pleased us, though I did not know then that October, 1914, marked my farewell to Prague and that I was leaving the city of my birth for good and would not see it again save for brief visits. Salzburg is a beautiful city, but never more beautiful than in the fall and early winter, the time we were stationed there. (Salzburg summers are spoiled by heavy rains and the influx of tourists.) The days were full of sunshine; the white, snow-capped mountains, and the green waters of the Salzach, contrasted with the deep, almost Mediterranean blue of the sky. The two banks of the Salzach cradle Salzburg, as the Moldau does in Prague. Salzburg resembles Prague also in its many churches, palaces, and gardens. Thus life and military service in Salzburg were not felt by us as too burdensome. We were allowed to have private quarters in the town and stayed in an ancient inn called Höllbräu (Hell-brew) in the narrow, quaint Judengasse. In the late afternoon we often played cards with our officers in the Café Tomaselli.

The famous *Festspiele,* inaugurated after the war by Max Reinhardt and Hugo von Hofmannsthal, had not started yet but the Mozarteum provided good music. On the eve of my departure for the front in early February, 1915, Weltsch and I attended a concert there by the great tenor Leo Slezak whom we had often heard in Prague. The concert is still vivid in our memories. The next day my company was sent to the Carpathian Mountains. Robert stayed behind in Salzburg. The war ended our almost daily companionship, which had begun in 1908, but not our close friendship.

IX

RUSSIA

Eₐʀʟʏ ɪɴ ᴛʜᴇ ᴡᴀʀ the Russians had occupied most of Austrian Galicia and threatened to cross the Carpathian Mountains onto the plains of Hungary. This would have meant that the road to Budapest and Vienna lay open to Russian armies. However, Austrian forces were able to stop the Russian advance on this front in 1915, and later on to force the enemy to retreat. (It was not until World War II that the Russians succeeded in crossing the Carpathian Mountains.) Warfare in the heavily wooded, rugged Carpathian foothills meant frontline combat amid snow, thaw, and mud, though it did not compare with the ferocity of the trench war on the Western front.

It was during this Carpathian campaign that I was taken prisoner, when the Russians staged a night attack on our position in the early hours of March 21, 1915. From then on, until January 12, 1920—for almost five years—I was to remain in Russia. These years brought for me a continuing personal encounter with three historical forces of our time—war, revolution, and colonialism. In many ways, I am inclined to regard my years in Russia as the decisive years of my life. They changed my

outlook and redirected my life into paths I could hardly
have foreseen in 1914.

Fate was kind to me. I had been exposed to only a few
weeks of actual infantry combat, and I had survived them
in good shape. When one is young and healthy, war becomes something of a personal physical contest, a challenge to daring. And so I found these weeks of war not
altogether unpleasant. Warfare on the Eastern front had
not yet become the mechanized mass slaughter it was to
become in the West. In the winter of early 1915, the optimistic mood of 1914 was still in the air, at least at the
front. We had not yet heard the stories of booming business conditions and war profiteering back home. I served
these weeks at the front conscientiously, without much
complaint or grumbling. Though I realized the absurdity
and futility of war, I did not then experience a strong reaction to them.

As prisoners of war, we were forced to march for eight
days along dusty Galician roads, from the Carpathian
Mountains to Lemberg, Galicia's capital, then in Russian
hands. This forced march gave me a foretaste of the Russian plain. We marched through the Polish and Ukrainian
countryside, and the villages we passed began to resemble
those of Russia rather than Bohemia. We met several Russian regiments on their way to the front. Their artillery
was excellent, but many of the soldiers lacked proper
shoes. The lopsided economic development of Russia, a
result of an industrialization stressing the defense need
of the state more than the welfare of its citizens, was visible even then. Still, these Russian troops, marching in
long columns and singing loudly, were an impressive sight.

Our first stop was Kiev, where we spent the Russian
Easter in a fortress high above the banks of the Dnieper

River. We saw nothing of the city, but we heard the pealing of the church bells in this "mother of Russian towns," and their ringing filled the air as incense does a church. From Kiev, we set out by slow train for far-off Samarkand. Thus it was that I had the good fortune of encountering Russia and Asia in this spring of 1915. Paradoxically, in this way I was to come to know the "mysterious" East before I knew the democratic West.

The trip revealed to me the immensity of the Russian empire. One reads about the vastness of Russia, yet one can only really experience it by traveling through it—and there is no better way than travel by train. (In this respect Russia resembles the United States.) In my trips across the broad Russian countryside I found the railroads comfortable. Even the third-class coach cars in which junior officers like myself then had to travel were not bad; though rather hard and crowded, they made tolerable overnight sleepers. The Russian passengers brought blankets and innumerable household possessions aboard, including the ubiquitous teakettle. (Free hot water was available at all stations and there was always a rush for it; the word *kipyatok,* "hot water," was one of the first Russian words we learned.)

I well remember the provincial railway stations and the heavy air of loneliness and boredom in the small towns where our train stopped between Samara on the Volga (the name of the city has since been changed to Kuibyshev) and Tashkent. The local people gathered there whenever a train was due; the station was their Corso and the train was their vicarious contact with the great outside world. The station master with his red cap looked important, and everyone waited for the three bells announcing the departure of the train.

I quickly came to like the Russian people and the Russian language. A long-suffering people who have long been ruled by tyrannical governments, the Russians nonetheless are full of vitality. They are deeply human, and in spite of their xenophobic, nationalist ideologies, are friendly and outgoing. There is a warmth in their personal relationships, a spontaneous need to communicate, which is in contrast with the greater reserve, the stronger insistence on privacy, I have found among most Western peoples.

Since I knew Czech, a Slavic language, it was fairly easy for me to learn Russian. Whereas Czech is a hard language (and the Czechs are the most efficient but not the most charming people among the Slavs), Russian is a very beautiful, soft language, without shrillness, which lends itself easily to song and poetry. Though I never became skillful enough in the language to appreciate all the subtleties of Russian poetry, I soon read prose easily. From Thomas Masaryk's two-volume *Russland und Europa: Studien über die geistigen Strömungen in Russland* (*Russia and Europe: Studies in Russia's Intellectual Development*) I knew of the passionate nineteenth-century debate about Russia's relationship to the West and her mission in the world. My reading in this field gave me the key to an understanding not only of Russian nationalism but that of all modern peoples who had to meet the challenge of the liberal West at various stages of their development—Spain and Germany, India, and the nations of Africa. After all, Russia was the first great non-Western civilization to undergo the process of Westernization. I came to appreciate better Masaryk's point of view that Russia had too little of the critical, pragmatic spirit of the West and too much of Dostoevsky's deep "spirituality" and superiority complex. Such attitudes partly explain the difficulties of so many countries in the twentieth century in transforming traditional regimes into modern free societies.

Before 1914, I had not traveled outside Central Europe; young people traveled then much less than they do today. Now, in 1915, the inscrutable wisdom of the Russian administration was carrying me thousands of miles into the heart of Asia, to Samarkand, one of the most ancient and storied cities of the Islamic East.

One of the first books I had studied in my Latin classes was an obscure biography of Alexander the Great, *De rebus gestis Alexandri Magni,* by a little-known author, Quintus Curtius Rufus. From reading this work, I remembered, and still do, the scene in which Alexander killed his close friend Cleitus in Samarkand (then called Maracanda) in 328 B.C. Later Samarkand had become a famous seat of Arab culture, until the city was finally destroyed in 1221 by Genghis Khan. Then his descendant Tamerlane made it the capital of his empire. Tamerlane and his grandson Ulug-Beg are responsible for most of the fabulous monuments and the opulent mausoleums and mosques which now adorn the city. It was in Samarkand that I got my first taste of an Oriental city. There was a colorful bazaar and innumerable narrow, winding streets flanked by completely walled-in houses, which had no windows facing the street but had charming courtyards which offered a cool, green, shaded retreat from the sun-baked streets.

The Russians had wrested Samarkand from the Emir of Bukhara in 1868 after a long siege, but in 1915 the native city still preserved the traditional way of life. At some distance from the native city a modern Russian city had been built, but there was little contact between the two. The

Russian city resembled a Russian provincial town, but was much neater than towns of similar size would have been in Russia. The Russians acted the part of masters and treated the natives without much consideration. The natives spoke a Turkish dialect, though their culture was derived from Arab and Persian influences.

Samarkand is a fertile oasis, formed by the river Zeravshan, which flows from the mountains on the Afghan border and loses itself in the desert a few miles beyond Samarkand, too weak to continue through the endless sands to reach Lake Aral. But Samarkand itself is an oasis of luxuriant green, irrigated by innumerable canals. After our arrival, we were housed in a summer training camp used by Cossacks who had left for the front. The camp was at the edge of the oasis and we could see the hairbreadth line which separated fertility from the awesome monotony of the desert. Medical conditions were primitive, and many of us suffered from malaria, enteric fever, and typhus. But otherwise life in the camp was not oppressive. We had our own internal organization. Food was plentiful and cheap. The guards, mostly peasants in their forties and fifties and too old for the front, were friendly. We were even allowed to go into town and move rather freely among the population. In the native city I found a number of Bukharian Jews, who spoke a Persian dialect and regarded themselves as descendants of the ten lost tribes, though they were probably remnants of the Babylonian captivity.

The realities of colonialism, which I saw in Samarkand for the first time, were unknown in Prague. (The Habsburg empire was the only great power in 1914 which had no colonies.) They made me sensitive to the difficulties that arise when a people try to govern peoples of another race and culture. In Prague there had been a bitter enmity, but it was one between nationalities that shared a similar racial and cultural background. Now in Samarkand I witnessed the clash of two different civilizations, a relationship not of rival peers but of master and subject, which expressed itself in countless ways. My thoughts went back to Alexander the Great who in a similar situation had recognized that intermarriage of Greek and barbarian was the only way of establishing peace and harmony among different peoples. Almost thirty years later, when I wrote *The Idea of Nationalism,* I praised Alexander for abandoning the narrow patriotism of his teacher Aristotle and becoming the first ruler to try to realize a vision of unity among mankind without distinction of descent or race. The Stoics and, later, St. Paul took up this vision. Lenin, too, had this vision in his early proclamations—at a time when nationalism in some parts of the world had assumed the narrow features of tribalism, with its insistence on common descent and even on purity of race. Lenin's Marxism never impressed or attracted me; his universalism did. (Of course, this universalism suffered by being framed in terms of a dogmatic creed which failed to recognize the pluralism of human society and the drive for self-determination in the individual.)

In February, 1916, I escaped from the prison camp and tried to make my way across the desert to Afghanistan. I did not succeed. After three days of exhausted wandering, I was recaptured. Now the camp authorities considered me a "dangerous" prisoner, and so they sent me to a remote spot deemed proof against any further escape attempts. It was a fortified outpost called Gultcha in the Pamir Mountains on the road to Kashgar, near the border of Chinese Turkestan. I was taken there by train. We traveled eastward through the fertile Ferghana valley, which is watered by the upper Syr Darya River (the Jaxartes of antiquity), to Andizhan, a cotton center at the end of the railroad line. From there we traveled thirty miles to Osh, a small Kirghiz town, the last populated center for many miles. This part of the trip was made in an ox-drawn cart with two very high wheels, enabling us to cross several river fords. From Osh to the outpost at Gultcha we went by horseback. My trip to Gultcha (and, later on, my return) was my only experience on horseback. Fortunately, the horses were small, intelligent Kirghiz horses, accustomed to find their almost invisible path over towering mountain peaks and along dangerous precipices.

This journey to Gultcha took five days, during which I had one of my worst malarial attacks but fortunately one of the last—the change of climate from the marshy lowlands of Samarkand to the 12,000-foot altitude of Gultcha apparently cured my illness. The guards who accompanied us, older Cossacks from Gultcha who once a week made the trip to Osh to collect mail and provisions, looked after me as best they could, so I survived the trip not too much the worse for wear.

During this month of March I had witnessed three springs; the first in Samarkand, before we left; the second in Osh, where we stayed for several days waiting for our escort; the third, a very timid and tender spring, in the high and rarefied air of Gultcha. There the late spring brought a thin layer of green to the slopes of the mountains, which lonely Kirghiz shepherds used as pastures. There were none of the mosquitoes which had plagued us in Samarkand. Instead, majestic eagles hovered overhead.

In Gultcha our small group of about ninety prisoners was cut off from all contact with the outside world. Yet the climate there during late spring was excellent, the quarters solid, and our time profitably spent in learning languages.

The natives of Turkestan were exempt from military service, but in the spring of 1916 the Russian government decided to mobilize them for labor service on the front. The Russians expected resistance from the natives and therefore decided to remove us "dangerous" prisoners to prevent our making common cause with native rebels. Thus in late June, 1916, we were ordered to set out by train from Andizhan to an unknown destination.

This new journey was to take thirty-two days in very slow trains and with frequent long halts before we reached our goal, first Samara on the Volga, and from there eastward on the trans-Siberian railroad to the farthest corner in far eastern Russia, the city of Khabarovsk on the lower Amur River. We crossed the Ural Mountains, and I was surprised to find that, at least in their southern part, they are not mountains but rather pleasant wooded hills with rich pasture grounds. The windows of our railroad cars were open. I still remember the fresh scent of the meadows and wildflowers as we moved eastward at snail pace (it is odd how one forgets events, people, books, and yet remembers some sensuous impressions). In spite of the presence of guards, a few of my fellow prisoners succeeded in escaping through the train windows. The consequence was that in Chelyabinsk we were transferred to cars with barred windows, used to transport criminals to Siberia. Next to each seat on the floor there were iron rings to which prisoners were once chained. We were no longer allowed to leave the cars at stations, and so we saw little of Siberia for the rest of the trip.

When we finally arrived at Khabarovsk we were still regarded as "dangerous" prisoners and were not allowed to mingle with the other prisoners there. We were put in special quarters, well-built houses normally used by the staff officers, but with four or five of us locked in each room. Except for our prison roommates and the guards, we saw no one.

The winter of 1916-1917 in Khabarovsk was rather hard because there was very little to eat—mostly unbuttered, dry macaroni and unsugared pressed tea, which the Russians called brick tea (*kirpichny tchai*), the cheapest kind of tea, which I have found nowhere but in Russia. But we were not alone in our distress. Although there was plenty of food in the countryside, the breakdown of the transportation system and the inefficiency of the administration—perhaps also the peasants' hostility to the cities and the war—prevented food from reaching most of Russia's industrial centers and the front. This poor food supply was one of the causes of the unrest which led to the March Revolution.

The March Revolution ended our solitary confinement. We were now allowed to join the other war prisoners. For me that meant the beginning of a new life. In the huge prison camps there were thousands of officers. Many of them were excited at the new turn in Russian politics and eager for intellectual contact. A large number of books were available, some sent to us by the Red Cross, some by relatives and friends. There were also several literary periodicals published in the camp. With some friends, I organized a series of lectures on a variety of subjects— philosophy, history, Russian literature and civilization. Our audiences were large and responsive. For many of them it was the first time they had been exposed to the life of the mind. After the war, of course, many of them again returned to their daily round of business and family life; yet for years after the war I met former prisoners who assured me how keenly they had enjoyed and still remembered the lectures they had heard in Siberia.

To be a prisoner of war involves many privations. A war prisoner is far from his family and home, from "normal" life; he is afraid of missing opportunities in his career and personal life that may never come again. But there is one compensation: A prisoner of war, at least if he is an officer, has an abundance of free time and the liberty to dispose of it according as he wishes. Paradoxically, he enjoys freedom. True, he is physically confined, but very few people, even outside prison camps, are completely free to move about and be wherever they wish at the moment. Duties and the limits of finances combine to restrict their freedom. But a prisoner of war is master of his own time; he may spend it reading good books, in conversation, or in thought and reflection.

I lost touch with most of my Siberian comrades after 1920, but two friendships lasted for life—that with Hanns Floch, who died in 1958 in San Francisco, and that with Hugo Knoepfmacher, who now lives in Washington. Both were born in Vienna, where I saw them frequently before 1938, the year they left to become Americans.

X

IDEOLOGICAL CONFLICT

THE MARCH REVOLUTION was neither planned nor organized. Lenin was in Switzerland when the revolution broke out. In a lecture he delivered to young socialists in Zurich in January, 1917, on the twelfth anniversary of "Bloody Sunday" (which marked the beginning of the revolution of 1905), Lenin stated that he was convinced he and the men of his generation (Lenin was then forty-seven years old) would not live to see the coming Russian revolution. He could only hope that the youth whom he addressed would be fortunate enough to take part in the coming proletarian revolution. Thus, to Lenin at least, the March Revolution was unexpected.

The March Revolution was a spontaneous outburst. It was prompted by the extreme inefficiency and corruption of the Tsarist regime, which by the beginning of 1917 had lost the war against Germany just as certainly as it had once lost the Crimean War and the Russo-Japanese War. The revolution was in part a revolt of hungry masses, in part a patriotic effort to improve Russia's military and civic strength. Outside the court circle there were few people in Russia who believed that Tsarist autocracy could continue. The old order in Russia did not succumb to revolutionary attacks, it crumbled and disintegrated from its own weakness. There was no moral or spiritual force to support it.

The March Revolution was greeted enthusiastically throughout Russia. Hopes ran high. Most people expected a utopia, though they had quite disparate concepts of what its nature would be. In Khabarovsk, people embraced each other in the streets. In our camp, military discipline noticeably weakened. The word "liberty," revered in Russia but only vaguely understood, had an almost mystical ring: The masses attributed magic power to it, and when the magic word failed to fulfill expectations, the people's immense hopes began to mingle with despair. The most urgent demand of the masses was for peace; that of the educated classes, for a more efficient pursuit of the war. The two demands were irreconcilable. This conflict only deepened the chaos and compounded the long-standing gulf between the "two nations" in Russia.

The present generation, which grew to maturity long after 1917, sometimes erroneously regards Lenin and his followers as the force that broke the tyrannical grip of Tsarist autocracy. In reality, the *ancien régime* collapsed weeks before Lenin arrived in Russia from exile. By the end of March, Russia, for the first (and last) time in its long history, was a free country. The police state was ended, the equality of all citizens and their political and civil liberties were proclaimed. But this free Russia, about to take its place at long last among modern European nations, lasted only a few months. Lenin's successful military coup, made possible by the chaos attending a lost war and the absence of a public consensus on self-government and liberty, put an end to liberty (and soon thereafter to the military chaos as well).

Lenin was helped to power by two factors. One was the continuous defeats of the Russian nation at war, to which he proclaimed his unconditional advocacy of peace; the other was the apocalyptic mood of part of the non-Bolshevik intelligentsia, who suspended all critical judgment and welcomed the revolution as a catharsis that would cleanse Russia (and, through Russia, mankind) of all its sins and failures. The modernization of Russian society was long overdue. However, there was no intelligent, efficient leadership from above, as there was in Japan after 1868, to guide the necessary transformation of a backward economy and social order. The Tsarist court was too corrupt; the educated classes, too doctrinaire and verbose; the peasantry, too backward and resentful of the cities and the intellectuals. These conditions were in no way unique to Russia—as in other peoples, they were complicated by a nationalist pride in the superiority of Russian ways.

Lenin, guided by a deep-seated, almost religious, conviction of the righteousness of the road he followed and supported by a close-knit, disciplined group of followers, oversimplified the issues and thus was able to appeal to the masses. His complete identification with the masses, his puritanism, his simplicity of dress and appearance, fortified his bid for leadership, just as similar traits did later in the case of Gandhi. But whereas Gandhi distrusted power, Lenin was eager for power—indeed, he overestimated its efficacy in changing human nature. His iron will to power also overcame the objections of conscience and doubt in the minds of Russian intellectuals.

Lenin saw his role as that of executor of universal historical laws; he did not share Napoleon's egocentric view.

However, like Napoleon, Lenin consummated, disciplined, and abolished the Revolution. More prudent than Napoleon, he restored and solidified the power of the Russian government and knew when to halt and bide his time. Napoleon was a Renaissance *condottiere*, humanized by the eighteenth century; Lenin was a nineteenth-century social scientist, made ruthless by the Russian mystique of revolution.

Of the three men who emerged on the world stage in the crucial years 1917-1920—Lenin, Gandhi, and Woodrow Wilson—only Wilson failed to communicate with the masses of his people. Wilson, like Lenin, was quick to comprehend that a global age was dawning and that national policy had to be guided by a new vision of mankind. As an American political scientist, he lived, not in the mystique of revolution, but in the mystique of the Western Protestant tradition of free men in a free society. In many ways, these two men anticipated the leadership which their nations were to exercise after 1945. By then, of course, they were dead—both died in 1924—and the Second World War ushered in a global era envisioned by Lenin and Wilson during the First World War. Part of this global vision was the independence of Asia, and of India, its heartland. Gandhi lived long enough to witness the beginning of its realization, but at the very moment of its achievement he fell victim to forces he himself had unwittingly helped to release. The tragic flaw in twentieth-century nationalism revealed itself not only in the American Congress' repudiation of Wilson's supranational vision but in the revolutionary mystique of nationalism, which was to prove as capable of a pseudo-messianic drive for power as was bolshevism.

The year 1917 marked the turning point in my generation's encounter with history. What had started as a traditional European war, based upon nineteenth-century ways of statecraft and patriotism, became a worldwide ideological conflict. The overthrow of tsarism, the March Revolution in Russia, the entry of the United States into the war—these events gave rise to high hopes for liberty and peace. On the other hand, the open assumption of Germany's leadership by the military headquarters under Hindenburg and Ludendorff confirmed the authoritarian character of the nation founded by Bismarck. The two great statesmen of nineteenth-century Europe, Bismarck and Gladstone, seemed to confront each other in the struggle for Europe's soul in 1917. At the same time, the war ceased to be a European conflict. It became, as Lenin so clearly understood, a world war and the beginning of a struggle for the mind of man everywhere. Japan staked out her claims in China and the Far East; the British promised independence to the Arabs if they rose against the Turks; Indian and African troops participated actively in all the battlefronts of Europe, Asia, and Africa. Thus the war stirred the "slumbering" East and aroused in its peoples the desire to be treated by the West as equal partners.

As the character of the war changed, the general mood of Europe changed, too. Many persons who in August, 1914, had been enthusiastic at the prospect of war, now felt a growing revulsion at the unprecedented suffering it had brought. A determination to end the terrible burden of war began to be heard in all nations. Now that the generation of 1914 is dying out, few may remember how strong was the outcry against war in 1917 and 1918; how much the war in that period anticipated the horrors of the Second World War; how it served as a prelude to the enormity of the evil genius of Hitler, who was deliberately to distort the history of the events of these years. But it is vital that these things be remembered by future generations.

In 1917, writers and poets no longer celebrated the grandeur of war and the heroism of battle. In 1916, Henri Barbusse published *Le feu,* a panorama of the reality of war suffered by the soldier in the trenches. The following year the German writer Leonhard Frank cried out (*"Der Mensch ist gut!"*—"Man is good!") against the inhumanity of war; from Switzerland Romain Rolland, who had just received the 1915 Nobel Prize in literature for *Jean Christophe,* with its moving depiction of Western Europe's mood before 1914, launched a series of pacifist manifestoes. (Tolstoy's great moral voice had been silenced by death in 1910; his disciple Gandhi had not yet begun to raise his voice to preach nonviolence. The personalities of the two men were complex and their politics were unorthodox, yet their pacifism and asceticism earned widespread public respect at a time of moral dissolution and growing violence.)

The world events of 1917 to 1920, which focused my attention on history, also made me a pacifist. As a pacifist, I was as little doctrinaire as I was in other respects. I followed a rather lonely path, as my conscience and my naturally limited understanding of the situation dictated. But from the First World War on, I distrusted power, officialdoms, and brass, and I abhorred the excesses of national pride and self-righteousness, the brutalization and inhumanity inherent in war. War represents the extreme case in which Kant's maxim to treat each man as an end in himself and Seneca's words *"Homo homini res sacra"* ("Man is a sacred object to man") cannot even be postulated. At that time, I would not have believed that in little more than another decade, the "spirit" of war and the spectacle of armed might would capture the minds of youth in Italy and Germany, and that still other peoples would succumb to fanatical militaristic nationalism.

Not only the agony of war (an agony which has little to do with the kind of weapons employed, despite the specter today of thermonuclear or "absolute" weapons), but also the brutality and excesses of revolution and counterrevolution, which I witnessed in Russia, repelled me. The March Revolution, which began in a spirit of hope and fraternity, soon led to a state of embittered suspicion and hatred. The life of man seemed to have returned to Hobbes's famous "state of nature," and become "solitary, poor, nasty, brutish, and short." Young men with rifles took the law into their hands. It became worse in the period of the civil war. It was this era of brutality in which the new Russia was born. Count Alexei Tolstoy, an aristocrat who returned to Russia from his years of exile in 1923 because he felt that the Bolshevik regime had saved the Russian nation and was building the foundations for a stronger Muscovite empire, has painted an unforgettable picture of the conditions of the period in *Darkness and Dawn* and *Road to Calvary*.

World War I and the Bolshevik Revolution showed me how thin is the veneer we call civilization, how close to the surface primitivism survives, how easily men reject the restraints imposed by civilization. Yet in World War I at least certain rules of civilized society were respected: As prisoners of war, we were protected by the Geneva

Convention, which most governments did honor. History has shown how important it ultimately is, even for the strong, to pay due regard to world public opinion and to observe international agreements. Civilized existence rests upon such restraints; barbarism is held in leash only by their presence. For that reason the world was shocked when, in August, 1914, the German Chancellor treated an international treaty as a mere "scrap of paper." Its contempt for and disregard of the moral force of world public opinion contributed to Germany's defeat in both wars, in spite of its great initial strength and victories. It is a lesson which needs to be learned by all nations.

But even the restraints of international agreements valid in war do not prevail in times of bitter revolutionary and counterrevolutionary conflicts when both sides are locked in a fanatical life-and-death struggle. Compromise is out of the question and any act, no matter how barbaric, is permissible. The "Red" terror during the Russian civil war was frightening, yet the "White" terror, with its disregard for human values, was even more savage and more depressing because it was not motivated by even the dedication to a universal cause that moved the Bolsheviks. Many people shuddered at the execution of the Tsar's family; but few of them cared about the countless other victims on both sides. Looking back on history, I am inclined to believe that this double standard has been the general rule. The brutalities of the country people in the Peasants' Wars could be explained by their long suffering and ignorance; their even more brutal repression by their masters was more revolting because this cruelty was deliberate and was undertaken in the name of order, civilization, and religion. The same was the case when ruling classes sup-

pressed colonial uprisings, or when the government of
Thiers savagely put down the Paris Commune. The ruling
classes have never attributed human dignity to peoples in
revolt, nor did they ever for a moment believe that the
life of one of the subject people could be equal to the
life of one of their own class or race.

I witnessed much of this inhumanity during the civil war
in Russia, particularly in Siberia, where I was imprisoned.
There, Admiral Alexander Kolchak, an ostensibly honor-
able and capable officer, the former commander of the
Black Sea fleet, was the head of the "White" Russian
armies. When the Communists seized power in Russia,
most observers believed their regime would not last long.
Organized resistance to them was strong, not so much
among the masses as among the articulate elements of the
population. Before long the new government's effective
control had been reduced to a fairly small territory in the
center of Russia, and it was surrounded on all sides by
"White" armies determined to overthrow Lenin's regime.
And for a time, in 1918, the "White" Russian armies,
fighting in the name of country, the Tsar, God, and religion, were also supported by expeditionary forces of the
Western allies. The importance of this intervention has
often been exaggerated. Its purpose was to try to restore
an effective "second" front in the East, which the Bolsheviks had ended by leaving the war and signing the
Treaty of Brest-Litovsk. Partly as a result of Russia's
surrender, the West was in a desperate position. Mutinies
had swept through the French army. The United States
had not yet completed the build-up of its forces. Thus, in
the Allies' eyes, the peace of Brest-Litovsk, which Lenin
concluded with Germany in March, 1918, appeared as a

betrayal. For formidable German armies were now freed
for a decisive offensive on the Western front. German victory seemed imminent.

It turned out otherwise. In early 1918, Germany was
too exhausted to carry its initially successful Western offensive to a decisive conclusion. At the time, of course,
the actual condition of the German armies was not known
to the West. It came as a surprise to the West when the
German front collapsed in the fall of 1918; this Western
victory freed Lenin from the burden of the Treaty of
Brest-Litovsk and helped restore Moscow's control over
Russia's Western borderlands. The halfhearted Allied
intervention at Murmansk and Arkhangelsk was soon
abandoned, for the Allies were too war-weary to continue
the campaign. But this retreat did not ensure the Communists' victory, as is sometimes stated. The major responsibility for Lenin's and Trotsky's victory rests with the
character of the "White" armies. The liberals and moderate
socialists who had opposed Lenin were soon eliminated
from the "White" governments and replaced by old-
fashioned reactionaries who did not understand the need
for change, much less a social revolution, and wished to
restore the vast estates seized by the Bolsheviks to their
former owners, and to reinstate Russian domination over
its subject peoples. The desperate effort to restore a dis-
credited *ancien régime,* the refusal to see its villainies and
follies, and to grant the Russian masses' longing for
equality and dignity doomed the "White" armies in spite of
their great initial advantages. Too many people in Europe
and the United States were unaware in 1918 how strongly
ideology had come to the fore in the wake of the war
and had taken hold of the lower classes and subject races.
The war caused a world revolution in the minds of people

all over the globe—in Russia as well as among Arabs, Indians, and Chinese. This revolution became visible only thirty years later, but it was already a factor in Russia in 1917 and soon became an important force in Asia, from Egypt to China, in the early 1920's.

XI

SIBERIA, JAPAN, AND EUROPE

I SPENT THESE crucial years in Siberia. In the general breakdown of ordered government that followed the Bolshevik coup, the prisoners of war in Khabarovsk commandeered a train in April, 1918, which carried us slowly westward, my second crossing of the immense expanse of Siberia. The authorities in the cities, where we stopped (often for days), were too preoccupied with local affairs to question our enterprise—the Treaty of Brest-Litovsk had just been concluded. However, when we arrived at Samara on the Volga, an officer ordered us to return to Siberia, in view of the civil war raging in the area west of the Volga. Some of the prisoners escaped, among them Hanns Floch, whose fiancée was anxiously awaiting him in Vienna. Hugo Knoepfmacher and I stayed on and were sent east again—this time to Novonikolaevsk (now Novosibirsk), on the Ob River. We were quartered in primitive barracks and remained there for seven months.

Meanwhile an event occurred which was to have considerable importance in my immediate future. Many Czech and Slovak war prisoners in Russia had formed a Czechoslovak Legion to fight against Austria-Hungary in the hope of achieving Czechoslovak independence. After Brest-

Litovsk, however, they could no longer continue to fight Austria on Russia's side since the Bolsheviks had taken Russia out of the war. So they decided to leave Siberia and make their way to the Western front. In the midst of military chaos, they were a well-organized, well-disciplined small army. This Czech Legion now gathered along the Siberian railway, from the Volga to Vladivostok, expecting transportation to Europe.

But instead of going to Europe, the Legion turned against the Communists in May, 1918, and quickly brought the whole Siberian railroad under its control. The Czechs used the excuse that they found their rear threatened by the Bolsheviks. The Bolsheviks, in turn, claimed the Legion was a tool of Western imperialism, and they accused the Czechs of making common cause with the "White" armies. The Legion, composed mostly of workers and peasants, was anti-Communist, but it also quickly became thoroughly disillusioned with the "Whites." Consequently, it held itself aloof from the civil war, though it too began to show disquieting signs of brutality in its actions.

The Czech Legion was hostile to the Austro-Hungarian prisoners of war, especially to the officers. After the Legion took over in Novonikolaevsk, we were not treated too well. At the end of 1918, in very cold, icy weather, our group was moved farther east to Krasnoyarsk on the Yenisei River, to a large camp with more than 10,000 prisoners. Prison life here was much better; during no other period of our imprisonment were our activities so well organized or our intellectual life as rich as it was here. We also enjoyed greater liberty in our contacts with the local population.

In April, 1919, I paid a brief visit to Irkutsk and got

in touch with the local Zionist organization, which was led
by a very capable and wealthy man, Moses Novomeysky,
whose father had helped open up the gold fields along the
Lena River after studying mining engineering in Germany.
He received me with typical Russian hospitality in his
home on Irkutsk's main thoroughfare. I became a regular
contributor to the local weekly *Yevreyskaya Zhizn* (*Jewish
Life*) and began to deliver lectures in Russian. Soon after
my return to Krasnoyarsk I decided to apply for Czechoslovak citizenship—the Habsburg monarchy had ceased to
exist months ago—and early in June, 1919, no longer a
war prisoner, I moved to Irkutsk, the headquarters of the
Czech Legion, where I joined the cultural and information
section as a civilian assistant librarian.

There I met Josef Kopta, a young officer, who later
became a well-known novelist and wrote a popular book,
Třetí rota, which dealt with the Legion's life in Siberia.
Kopta, a very pleasant man and a good liberal, was the
editor of an independent hectographed paper *Vykřik*
(Outcry). It was written in the spirit of optimistic, pacifist
libertarianism, very much along the lines of Central
European Expressionist publications of the day. I collaborated with Kopta on the paper, writing on Gustav
Landauer, Walt Whitman, and others. If copies of *Outcry*
survive, they will bear witness to our fervent though con-
fused hopes in 1919, our overestimation of the power of
good intentions, our refusal to face the unpleasant realities
of human nature and the follies of governments. Since
then I have learned many lessons: I am more resigned and
have, I think, perhaps, acquired a better sense of humor.
But in this fleeting moment in 1919, like many of my
generation then in their twenties, I resembled Don Quixote, trying to defend the weak, the helpless, and the

oppressed. Don Quixote may seem ludicrous, but amid the general moral, spiritual, and social corruption into which Spain had sunk at the end of the sixteenth century, the Knight recalled the vision of a better humanity.

During these months in 1919 I felt closer to Kopta than to my other acquaintances in Irkutsk. Soon after his return from Siberia he married a beautiful girl from a small Czech town. In 1923, when I stayed in Prague for several weeks to take the final examinations ("rigorosa") for my doctorate, which the outbreak of the war had prevented me from doing in 1914, I enjoyed the company of this pleasant, handsome couple. I saw the Koptas again in Prague years later, in 1937. A decade after that, when I returned in 1946, I found that neither his wife's beauty nor his talent had withstood the wear and tear of those difficult times. After the Communist take-over of Czechoslovakia, Kopta's life ended in long illness and lonely poverty. Yet, even in 1947, when he was drinking more than he should, his open, friendly manner reflected his inner probity. Though he may not have been a great writer, he was a great human being, good-humored, tolerant, and understanding.

My stay in Irkutsk was a profitable one. Irkutsk was then the largest town in Siberia, a very livable and pleasant city of about 100,000 inhabitants. It had little of the drowsy atmosphere, the boredom, or the commonplace appearance of the typical Russian provincial town. One could hardly imagine Chekhov's three sisters in Irkutsk longing so desperately for Moscow. The city was nearly three hundred years old. A century before it had been the center of trade with China and North America; now it was again expanding rapidly. A university had recently been founded there. The people of Irkutsk were descendants of pioneers, rebels, political prisoners, and fugitive serfs, and were a self-reliant and proud populace. Even their standard of living seemed to me higher than in Penza and similar cities where we had stopped for several days in 1915.

In these troubled months of 1919, cultural life in Irkutsk went on; the stores were well kept; the pastry shops and tearooms, inviting; the streets, wide, clean, and tree-lined. The city was full of stately wooden houses, built to withstand the rigors of the climate; their doors and window frames were often beautifully carved, and behind their large double windows plants and flowers were displayed. The city was located on the Angara River, which connects nearby Lake Baikal with the Yenisei River and the Arctic Sea. The Angara with its cold, clear, swift, green water reminded me of the Salzach in Salzburg. In many ways, the fall of 1919 was as lovely as that of 1914 had been, though the world was now a far different place and I had learned much.

Siberia's climate has a sinister reputation that it does not deserve, at least not that of southern Siberia. The summers, it is true, are unpleasantly hot; heavy winds blow in the dust from the *taiga,* the swampy, coniferous forest region of Siberia; and there are swarms of mosquitoes. But the spring and fall, though short seasons, are marvelous, and I thought of them years later when I encountered similar seasons in New England. The Siberian winters were not bad. The snow comes very early in the fall; it does not melt but remains white and crisp. The air is brisk and invigorating. The sun shines most of the day and the sky is bright blue. If one dons heavy felt boots, a peasant sheepskin, and a fur cap, and covers the exposed parts of his face with grease, he can enjoy the brittle, dry cold outdoors. On winter evenings my room was well heated, there was wood in abundance, and the mild light of the study lamp and the muted humming of the ever-boiling, ever-ready samovar created an atmosphere conducive to long hours of reading and—in the very last weeks, when Knoepfmacher joined me in Irkutsk—of discussion. There was also much else to do in the evening: lectures in Czech and Russian, concerts, and plays. I still remember the very fine performances there of Chekhov's *Uncle Vanya* and *Three Sisters*. (Of the several *Three Sisters* I have attended, this Irkutsk performance and a presentation in Paris of Pitoeff's translation on Whitsunday, 1960, stand out in my memory.) Though I do not much like folk art (which is so much favored in the Soviet Union today), I also visited, out of curiosity, the Buryat theater (the Buryat are a Mongol Buddhist people living south of Lake Baikal), where I met several Buryat students who struck me as very bright and eager for Western learning.

In Irkutsk, then far behind the front, the local administration in 1919 was relatively liberal. The presence of the Czechoslovak Legion helped to assure this freer atmosphere. But in mid-November, Omsk, Admiral Kolchak's capital, fell to the Communists, and it was clear that there were no "White" armies strong enough to stop the Communists now. So when I learned that my mother was dying of cancer, and having received some money from Europe, I decided to leave Siberia via Vladivostok and return home.

My trip back to Europe was a rather difficult one. During the summer, Irkutsk was connected with its railroad station on the opposite bank of the Angara River by a pontoon bridge. In winter one could cross the river on the ice. But between these seasons there were weeks when only small rowboats, steadily endangered by drifting ice floes, were the only link the city had with the outside world. In such a boat Knoepfmacher and I crossed the Angara. I took the trans-Siberian train; Knoepfmacher later made his way across Mongolia to Shanghai.

The territory east of Lake Baikal around Chita was held by Cossack forces commanded by a tyrannical leader, Ataman Grigori Semyonov, who hated the Czechs and who loved to torture and execute those he captured. Fortunately, we passed through the danger zone unharmed and reached the great Manchurian city of Harbin. After three days in Harbin, which had come to resemble a Russian city since it was so full of Russian *émigrés,* I arrived at Vladivostok, a beautiful port city that reminded me of Naples and Hong Kong. From there I sailed with two other former war prisoners from Prague on a Russian boat bound for Tsuruga, a small port on Japan's west coast. Our departure was a bitterly cold one; an icy wind was blowing, and the harbor was frozen, so that an ice-breaker had to precede our steamer for about four hours. Thirty hours later we landed in Japan; it was raining and there was neither ice nor snow.

It was now January, 1920. Almost four years and ten months had passed since I had entered Russia in March, 1915. Behind me the "White" front had collapsed in chaos; Kolchak fell into Communist hands at Irkutsk and was executed at the beginning of February, 1920. An age-old chapter of Russian history, the regime of the Tsars, was now closed forever. If one could single out among the many causes for its tragic end the most important cause, it would be the Tsarist regime's ineptitude and senseless cruelty, its haughty refusal to understand, and to accommodate itself to the changing spirit of the times.

Japan offered a picture in marked contrast to the character of Russia. Starting from scratch, a capable elite, willing to learn and to accommodate, had in forty years transformed this medieval, self-isolated realm into a modern industrial state. I was impressed by the orderliness of Tsuruga, Yokohama, and Tokyo, by the fact that even the ricksha coolies waiting for clients read newspapers, by the cleanliness and efficiency of the trains. Japan seems to me—and I speak as a layman—an unusually gifted but imitative nation. In the age when Bismarckian militarism was triumphant, Japan imitated Prussia; in the 1920's, it took as its model the dominant democracies; in the 1930's, it adopted fascism when that way of life seemed to represent, in the minds of many Europeans, the wave of the future.

We stayed five weeks in Japan, seeing much of its beauty, above all lovely Kyoto. We were quartered in a hostel run by the American Joint Distribution Committee while we waited for boat space, which was still at a premium. Finally we got a cabin on a very old Pacific and Orient steamer, a slow freighter which carried second-class passengers, most of them missionaries returning after the war years to England. Fortunately, the boat made long stops in Shanghai, Hong Kong, Penang (where we visited nearby Kuala Lumpur) and Colombo (with an excursion to Kandy). Then after sailing slowly up the Red Sea, we landed at Marseilles late in March, 1920. From there we crossed Switzerland and southern Germany to the new Czechoslovak border town of Fürth in the Böhmerwald. A few hours later my father met me at the Prague railroad station. Siberia, where I had lived for several momentous years, and the beauty of the Far East, of which I had caught impressive glimpses, now lay far behind me. But I hoped that someday I would revisit these distant lands, to recall my youth, to report on changes; alas, like so many other hopes and dreams, this, too, has remained unfulfilled.

Nothing of what I saw in the weeks following my return was much of an inducement to stay in Central Europe. Prague, now a capital city, had lost much of its captivating quiet charm. The new Czechoslovak government was building on faulty foundations: It identified the new state with a single ethnic, linguistic group, at the expense of the other groups living in what was now the new Czech state. A similar narrow nationalism had taken hold in the whole of Central Europe. In Germany, the arrogant nationalism that had prevailed ever since Bismarck's triumph seemed only to have grown in virulence. The collapse of Bismarck's Reich only twenty years after the death of its founder did not induce many Germans to re-evaluate the foundations laid by the "Iron Chancellor" in his contempt for democracy. On the contrary, the majority of Germans insisted on the continuance of Bismarck's Berlin-centered Reich and hoped to undo Germany's defeat and to reassert German superiority, particularly against the "inferior" Slavs on its eastern borders. In Central Europe the experiences of the war had in no way lessened the nationalism which had led to the war. Quite the contrary. Thus the prospects for democracy and peace appeared dim.

A decade earlier, I had expected to live my life in Prague; in 1920, I now felt something unhealthy and restrictive in the unsettled atmosphere of Central Europe. So I decided to pay a visit to my friend Robert Weltsch in Berlin. That city had just lived through the Kapp *Putsch,* engineered by old-fashioned Prussian conservatives; after its failure it was followed by a leftist workers' uprising in the Ruhr, which, in turn, had been cruelly suppressed by the Reichswehr. My stay with my friend Robert was a delightful one—the easy harmony and tacit understanding had survived our five years of separation. But Berlin seemed to me a place where the defeated authoritarian order had been replaced not by liberty but by license.

Back in Prague once more, I became restless. My mother, who had undergone an operation for cancer of the breast in 1910, had suffered a relapse in 1918. She knew she was dying, but she bore her often excruciating pain uncomplainingly, with dignity and serenity. The war years had been difficult for her as for so many mothers. I was thousands of miles away in prison camps (which in the imagination seemed worse than they were) and letters took several months to reach their destination. My brother Fritz, two years younger than I, was serving on the front in an artillery unit. Fortunately, he, too, returned home unharmed after his years of dangerous service. My youngest brother, Franz, and my only sister, Grete, who had been children when I left, were now in their teens.

My mother's thoughts were absorbed in the future of her children. I had many talks with her, but there seemed to be an invisible barrier between us; her life was ending, mine was beginning. I tried to reassure her, but what assurance can well-intentioned youth give to the old and dying? A few weeks after I departed from Prague for Paris she died peacefully in her sleep; before this last sleep claimed her, my father heard her repeating time after time the names of her four children.

After leaving Prague in May, 1920, I revisited the city regularly to see my family and friends. My brother Fritz, in many ways the most remarkable member of the family, was unlucky in his business ventures. His longing to emigrate to Palestine as a member of the Kvutza Beth

Alpha was not fulfilled. He was burdened by his daily affairs and probably found his greatest happiness in his marriage. He, his wife, and their older son later perished during the German occupation; his younger son, Leo, succeeded in escaping to England, and later returned as a member of the Czechoslovak army and married a Czech Catholic girl, Mařenka. They now live in Czechoslovakia with their son Michael, named after Leo's brother. Thus one branch of the family still has its roots in Prague, a fact which would certainly please my father.

When the Germans overran Central Europe in the late Thirties my brother Franz and my sister Grete, with her son who was born in Budapest, came to the United States. (The son has since forgotten his Hungarian, has attended Yale and Syracuse Universities, and has married a girl from a southern Protestant family; they now live in Boston with their two daughters.) Franz has had an unusually happy marriage for thirty-five years and has established himself successfully in New York City. He is the only one of the family who still feels some ties to Prague. As for myself, I left my homeland in the fall of 1914, and my subsequent returns have been only brief visits. I have lived in many places since, and I felt at home in all of them. I never longed for any of them once I left, though I remain grateful to them for the opportunity they gave me of feeling at home in their midst, of meeting people, of broadening my understanding.

My father understandably did not approve of my leaving Prague. He wished me to settle there, as a lawyer or scholar, and to marry well, which meant to him the daughter of a "good," well-to-do Prague family. But I went abroad to work in Zionist organizations, despite his low opinion of Zionism and Zionists. I left without a penny, and for years my income was less than modest. I married a young woman without money or dowry, again to my father's disappointment. He shook his head when I emigrated to Palestine in 1925, and again when, in 1929, I gave up my relatively secure position there and, now the head of a family and no longer young, started the long search for a new home and new work. But he never opposed or criticized my steps. With his old-fashioned chivalry, he accepted his daughter-in-law and soon came to like her. As a man of little formal education, he was proud that I was a writer (between 1922 and 1931 I wrote eight books); that, when I came to Prague, he could attend my lectures and share in the audience's approval of them. Of my life and problems, he knew very little and consequently he tended to overestimate my "success." My father died in 1931, a few days before I was to sail to the United States to start a new life. A surprisingly large number of people turned out for the funeral, many of whom I had not seen since before 1914. For he was generally well liked. To quote the German poet Mathias Claudius, "He was a good man . . . and he was my father."

XII

THE TWILIGHT OF IMPERIALISM

DURING THE YEARS from 1920 to 1931 I lived in Paris, London, and Jerusalem. Though my family and I lived in very modest circumstances in this period, it never bothered me. Apparently, in this respect, I had little of the "bourgeois" in my make-up. Even more important, I never felt that I was in exile during these years of *Wanderschaft*. I felt fully at home in these cities and lands. I did not share Dante's famous bitter lament about exile:

> Tu proverai si come sa di sale
> Lo pane altrui, e com' è duro calle
> Lo scendere e il salir per l'altrue scale.

("You will find out how salty the bread tastes in foreign countries and how hard it is to climb and descend stairs in alien lands.")

Heinrich Heine, the great German poet and patriot, shared Dante's experience. Living in Paris, then the cultural capital of Europe and far more beautiful than any contemporary German city, Heine still longed for Germany. Two years before his death, Heine explained why, though he had lived in France for a quarter of a century, he had not become a French citizen: "I could never free myself from a certain dread that I should do anything which might seem, even if only partly so, to be breaking away from my native land."

Years later I was to encounter many refugees from Hitler's racial madness who felt that they had gone into "exile" in Western Europe or in the United States. They not only compared their new residence unfavorably, sometimes contemptuously, with their "lost" homeland, but were full of pity for themselves and their fate. They were, I think, a minority but they were frequently a vocal one. Fortunately, as I have said, I have never felt myself a stranger wherever I have been—in Russia, in France, in England, or in Palestine.

When I arrived in Paris in May, 1920, it was a city resplendent with its recent victory. It was not the nervous, tense city of 1937, nor the shoddy, depressed Paris of 1946, nor the energetically rebuilding Paris of 1962—all of which I was to see later. In 1920, the mood of *la belle époque* still survived in its magnificent *parcs* and *palais*. But Paris was a very old city, old not only in the glorious monuments of its past but in the houses where its people lived, houses without modern conveniences, houses with an aura of decrepitude and neglect. The center of Paris had changed little over the decades. Modern times seemed to have bypassed its ancient streets and structures. I lived in a hotel, mostly used by students, in the Rue Cujas, near the Boulevard St. Michel. The Jardin du Luxembourg and the Sorbonne were just around the corner. Though I worked in the center of the right bank, on the Place Édouard VII, near the Opéra and the Boulevard des Capucines, my home was the Boulevard St. Michel, the Boulevard Montparnasse, and the Rue Richelieu (site of

the Bibliothèque Nationale). Before coming to Paris, I had
read much of Anatole France and Zola; now I discovered
La Nouvelle Revue Française and *Le Vieux Colombier,*
the *bouquinistes* along the Seine and the bookshops near
the Odéon; I also discovered Charles Péguy, Sorel, Proudhon, and the generation of the Dreyfus affair, Charles
Maurras and Maurice Barrès, Daniel Halévy and Romain
Rolland, Roger Martin du Gard and André Spire. I became well acquainted with Spire and Jean Richard Bloch,
and I was the first to write about them in German.

I was impressed with the importance of the *hommes des
lettres*, of the intellectuals in French life; again and again
they had spoken up as *la voix de la conscience du monde,*
something unknown in Germany. They had made their
voice heard during the Dreyfus affair, and they had won
the battle against blind chauvinism and emotional nationalism, against the entrenched forces of the army and the
Church. But I also learned that democracy was not as
firmly established in France as it was in England or the
United States. Like the Germans, the French seemed always in danger of succumbing to the lure of the man on
horseback, to the myth of *la grande nation*, with one important difference, however: French common sense ultimately prevailed, and their grandiose aspirations were
backed by a culture with a universal appeal. That the
French often did not live up to or abused it for selfish ends
did not lessen the image of *la belle France* in the eyes of
those longing for liberty and equality.

The great creative age for France was the eighteenth
century, with the humanism of the Enlightenment. The
majority of the French never repudiated this heritage,
whereas the majority of the Germans after 1815 rejected
the wisdom of the *Aufklärung*. Of course, there were many

Frenchmen, not only in the army and the Church, but also among the intellectuals from De Maistre to Maurras, who rejected everything the year 1789 implied as contemptuously as many Germans did.

Charles Péguy and his *Cahiers de la Quinzaine* became my special discovery that year. Péguy fascinated me because as a socialist, a republican, a Christian, and a nationalist he was an entirely unorthodox figure, an *Einzelgänger*, a "loner," for whom neither Church nor party was the authority, and who, after his apprenticeship in the Dreyfus affair, struck out for himself in a spirit of fierce independence and monastic dedication. He was killed in the Battle of the Marne in 1914, at only forty-one years of age. By 1920 he was almost forgotten; then the 1930's discovered the socialist and Dreyfusard, the 1940's, the patriot and the Christian, the 1950's, the poet. For me his most fascinating essay was *Notre jeunesse*—I am sorry that I know of no complete English or German translation of it. The conflicts which Péguy discussed were made real for me each morning because I regularly read *Action Française*, the lively organ written by Maurras, Léon Daudet, and Jacques Bainville (though its vitriolic attacks on the Republic became monotonous after a time). The other French papers seemed vacuous and boring to me, with the exception of the short-lived *Oeuvre* and the afternoon *Le Temps*, which was revived more brilliantly in *Le Monde* after 1945. I began to understand that France was not a fully cohesive modern nation, and that there were, in fact, *"les deux Frances."* Consequently, I was not surprised, later, in 1934, in 1940, and in 1958, to see the strong hold fascism and communism exerted over many Frenchmen and the scant respect many felt for parliamentary democracy and constitutional legality. Still, the French had the saving grace of political humor so well represented in *Le Canard Enchainé.*

I lived in Paris for fifteen months. Since I had little money for travel, I was not able to see much of France; instead I explored the city itself and its environs. I seldom went to art galleries, though I knew a number of painters. I also found the orchestras and the Paris Opera inferior to those in Vienna, Prague, or Berlin. But I enjoyed the theater, for it opened up to me the whole world of French dramatic literature from the seventeenth-century classics to Claudel and Vildrac. In no other city have I attended the theater as frequently as I have in Paris, not only when I lived there but during my frequent visits from 1922 to 1962. French literary life in the early 1920's was much superior to that of later decades. We eagerly awaited each new issue of *La Nouvelle Revue Française.* Proust, Gide, Giraudoux, Valéry, Claudel, Julien Benda, Romain Rolland, Suarès, Roger Martin du Gard, Mauriac, Jules Romains—to name a few writers of very different talent and importance—were all in their creative period, and younger man like Montherlant and Malraux were preparing to enter the scene. Compared with such creativity, the present state of literature in France, as in Britain, Germany, and the United States, seems far less rich—though perhaps this is in the perspective of one looking back at some of his happiest years, and posterity may judge differently.

There were aspects of Parisian life I did not like and liked even less when I looked back to France from Britain or the United States: above all, the intellectual poverty and venality of most of the metropolitan press and the near-police-state atmosphere that allowed censorship of the press. These and other unpleasant tendencies pervaded

Parisian life and recalled Central Europe rather than the West. Police-state tactics were practiced on a small but annoying scale by the *concierges* in the houses. The bureaucratic procedure in all police precincts included police visits during the night to cheaper hotels—I lived in one —to inspect passports and permits of sojourn. The attitude of Parisians toward the police was unfriendly, often hostile (it was perhaps an outgrowth of the rigid class consciousness and hostility separating the upper bourgeoisie and the proletariat). All these things seemed to me to make France more like Italy and Spain than like Britain or the United States. This may have changed after 1945, but in the 1920's and 1930's it was as pervasive an element of Parisian life as was its eroticism, which consisted as much of acting out an accepted reputation as anything else. The open manifestations of love in parks and on the streets, though "natural" in Paris in 1920, were then unknown, for example, in London; yet when I returned to London in 1945, I was astonished to find how much like Paris London had become in this respect.

I visited London for the first time in the early summer of 1920. There was much squalor but also grandeur in which an afterglow of Edwardian magnificence still prevailed. In London I once more met Robert Weltsch, and we spent much time talking over politics and our personal lives. Robert was about to marry a young woman from southern Bohemia whom he had met during the war. I also saw an old friend from my Bar Kochba days, Leo Herrmann, who was now an official in the Zionist organization. It was at his house that I met his sister-in-law, Yetty Wahl. She had been brought up in Berlin, had left in 1919 to work in the Zionist office in Copenhagen, and a year later had been transferred to London.

In the early fall Yetty and I became engaged, and on April 16, 1921, we were married in Paris, in the *Mairie* of the Fifth Arrondissement, opposite the Panthéon. Our wedding banquet was a luncheon in a *crémerie* near the Luxembourg Gardens, and in the afternoon we took our "honeymoon" trip to the forest of Fontainebleau. In the evening Yetty moved into my room in the Rue Cujas—like all such rooms, it had a large double bed—until she had to return to her work in London. At the end of the summer of 1921, I followed her to London. We lived in London for the next four years in two furnished rooms, first on Belsize Road, near Swiss Cottage, then on Upper Park Road, near Belsize Park. Our quarters were modest, but they were better than our one room in the Rue Cujas.

The office where Yetty and I worked was in Great Russell Street, a few steps from the British Museum and some fascinating bookshops that specialized in the Middle and Far East. English literature and theater never interested me in the same way that French literature and the Paris theater did; on the other hand I found the British way of life and the political atmosphere of London more congenial. I had a feeling of security in Britain that I had not experienced in Central Europe or in France. London in the early 1920's was the center of a worldwide political, financial, cultural complex; everywhere one met persons who had spent long years of service abroad, and there were many students from Asia and Africa. The Parisian journals concentrated on France (and often, on Paris) and despite their literary perfection and intensity were rather provincial in this respect; the British periodicals, while inferior in literary and artistic merit, took the whole world for their subject matter.

But even the British did not realize they were witnessing

the turning point in modern history. They thought, as did the French and the Americans, that they were still living in the world that had existed before 1914. The war itself was forgotten in a zestful pursuit of pleasure, in a misinterpretation of life and history. Few were aware of the profound revolution that had taken place in the minds of peoples all over the globe, or that this revolution would express itself one day soon in the reordering of national and international society.

The United States, too, reverted to its old ways. It soon reaffirmed its isolation, in spite of Wilson's speeches on his Western trip in September, 1919. Wilson warned his countrymen, with uncanny foresight, of the consequences of abandoning the Treaty of Versailles, but to no avail. Britain, faithful to past political tradition, still focused its attention on signs of French "militarism," unaware of the much greater danger from Germany. France, upset by the refusal of its Allies to ratify a treaty of alliance to prevent renewed German aggression, acted out of neurotic insecurity. Fascist Italy, oblivious of realities, itched to enter the great imperial power game. The fascist infection began to spread throughout Central Europe and the Balkans, where a reactionary elite wished to perpetuate an obsolete social order under the pretext of defending society—which meant the status quo—and the Church, which might have found more worthy defenders than Horthy, Dollfuss, or Pilsudski. The democracy which triumphed in 1918 seemed destined to become only a brief interlude. The foundations of Western society had been profoundly shaken. The German and Italian nationalists and the Russian Communists knew it. But Great Britain and the United States remained unperturbed.

My experiences in Turkestan, and my interest in Pales-

tine, led me to question the generally accepted premise
that the colonial empires established around 1900 by the
nations of Europe and the United States would last. The
end of the war had brought a new scramble for the spoils
of empire. Britain, by gaining German East Africa, fulfilled Rhodes's dream of a trans-African Cairo-to-Cape-
town link. Britain also thought to hold Egypt, promised
Palestine to the Zionists, and secured the land route across
Arabia to India as well as the oil to be found along the
route. France enlarged her African holdings and realized
in Syria and Lebanon the aspirations of the Crusaders,
which she claimed as her heritage. The United States,
while looking askance at European "imperialism," com-
peted with British oil interests, kept a tight rein on Cuba,
Puerto Rico, and the Philippines, and took a dim view of
the socialist revolution in Mexico, finally intervening with
armed forces in 1916.

I was one of those who saw that the "unchanging" East
was changing rapidly under the impact of modern Western
civilization and that Britain's liberal tradition, the fountainhead of freedom in Europe and North America, was
transforming the world. My years in Britain made me an
admirer of her political wisdom and sense of fair-dealing,
but a critical admirer, because all of us, English and non-
English alike, are imperfect and fallible human beings.
Even so, I have remained faithful to my Anglophilia.

I spent much of my free time in the reading room of the
British Museum. I could not, of course, cover the whole
field of Asia, Africa, and Latin America in my research.
Personal preference, as much as the limitations of the
material accessible to me, made me confine my study to
the Middle East, from Egypt to India. The result of these
years of reading and research in London and later in

Jerusalem was my volume *A History of Nationalism in the East,* which was published in Germany in 1928. It had its shortcomings and it tried to cover too much; my next two books, *Nationalism and Imperialism in the Hither East* and *Western Civilization in the Near East,* were more specialized and better in their details. Even so, *A History of Nationalism in the East* was a pioneer study in a field which was to attract widespread attention thirty years later as a central aspect of the world revolution of our time. It was widely read in India, even by Jawaharlal Nehru, who noted it when he told the history of the Indian national movement in his autobiography. I was also fortunate in having this book, as well as the three that followed it, translated into English and published by Routledge in London. The book has been out of print for well over twenty years, yet its basic premises are as valid in the 1960's as they were in the 1920's. Having shifted my interests elsewhere many years ago, I was glad to find the book singled out in the authoritative *Select Bibliography: Asia, Africa, Eastern Europe, Latin America,* published in 1960 by the American Universities Field Staff under Phillips Talbot, as "a rewarding study, remarkable in its prescience of nationalism and achievements in the area from Egypt to India."

Thus I learned in London not only of Britain but of the world. Britain and Russia are the frontier powers of Europe. They look not only to the European continent but out upon the world. Britain is the heartland of the modern West, where individual liberty and modern pluralistic society originated; Russia is the link between the East and West, belonging fully to neither and continuing a pattern of doctrinal orthodoxy and centralized authoritarianism alien to the modern West. It was my good fortune to spend over four years in Russia and nearly as long a time in England. Paris was a welcome esthetic interlude. Russia and Britain, in different ways, deepened my understanding of history. Whereas most of continental Europe was to move in the direction of fascism and war, in Britain a nondoctrinaire democratic socialism and pacifism were growing. Yet Britain was the only major power to take the initiative in the struggle against Hitler— the Soviet Union and the United States waited until they were attacked or until Hitler declared war upon them— and the British fought alone for many months, with uncommon courage.

Before 1914, it was almost unthinkable that socialists or labor parties would take part in European governments. The dogma of class war dominated the mind of the propertied class even more than that of the workers. The world revolution of the twentieth century changed this state of mind. After the war, industrial and agricultural productivity increased greatly, and in advanced countries the traditional economy of scarcity was being replaced, for the first time, by an economy of abundance; the conscience of the upper classes awakened from its traditional self-satisfaction; the workers abandoned the Marxist myth of their permanent status as the exploited proletariat that only revolution could transform. This change in attitudes occurred more smoothly and speedily in Britain and in Scandinavia than on most of the European continent. It was beginning during the years I lived in London.

In spite of great economic difficulties, to men of good will it seemed possible to prevent future wars and to assure greater social justice. The Labour party was rapidly growing. Only twenty years earlier, in 1900, the year of its founding, the Labour party had elected its first two

members to the House of Commons. In the last election
before the war—that of 1910—Labour won forty-two
seats. After the war, the election in early 1923 saw 159
Labour representatives win seats, and in November of the
same year the party increased its number to 191. These
were stirring times for all friends of social reform. The
first Labour government entered office as a minority
government dependent on Liberal support. It lasted only
nine months, but to quote the *Encyclopædia Britannica,*
it "disposed quite sufficiently of doubts whether Labour
could govern. The ministers not only did well in public,
they also earned the good will of their departmental staffs."

I still remember the excitement of the period. I had
joined the Fabian Society and the Hampstead branch of
the Independent Labour Party, which officially included
J. Ramsay MacDonald. The great days of these two organizations were already in the past—the *Fabian Essays*
had appeared in 1889, and Keir Hardie, the first leader of
the I.L.P., was dead—but the formation of the first Labour
government seemed the fruit of these pioneering ventures.
Now trade unionists and socialists were sitting in the seats
of the mighty, and on the whole they were accepted by
the British civil service and managers of Britain's indus-
tries without the opposition other socialists found in Germany and France. The strength of the democratic process
in the few countries where democracy was a way of life
was surprising.

At the end of 1923 a mass meeting to celebrate
Labour's success was held in Queens Hall (it has since
been destroyed by the war, but was then the home of the
Promenade Concerts, which we often attended, conducted
by Sir Henry Wood, who did so much to acquaint the
English public with good music). George Lansbury—an

ardent Christian Socialist who had done exemplary work
in London's slum district of Poplar and who later became
leader of the Labour party in 1931, after MacDonald's
defection—introduced Mrs. Annie Besant to the audience,
calling her his teacher. Lansbury was then sixty-four years
old; Mrs. Besant was seventy-six, but still a very powerful
speaker. In the heyday of Victorian morality, she had
pioneered for socialism, birth-control, and free thought;
then she turned to theosophy, went to India, revived Indian pride in Hindu mysticism, founded the Central Hindu
College in Benares, became the first champion of Indian
home rule, and in 1917 was elected president of the Indian National Congress. Standing there on the platform,
she could contrast the far-off days of forty years ago when
she had been a radical agitator and strike leader before
joining the Fabian Society in 1885, with her preoccupa-
tion, now, of having discovered in a Hindu youth, Krishna-
murti, the vehicle of a new Messiah. Since I was interested
in India, I met Mrs. Besant, but her faith in occult forces
made understanding difficult. Her biographers have called
her "the passionate pilgrim" and referred to her "strange
lives"; yet in her very strangeness she represented an
aspect of English character that is often overlooked: a
mixture of the practical with a yearning for the exotic, and
a dedication to the faith of the reformer.

Lansbury could understand Mrs. Besant better than I
could, for his faith in Christianity was as strong as hers in
Hinduism. His Christianity made him one of the most
beloved Socialist leaders in Britain—again a typical British
attitude, unthinkable among continental socialists—and at
the same time a staunch pacifist. It was on this issue that
in 1935 he departed from the leadership of the Labour
party, which came out in favor of resistance to fascism.

Lansbury, who was then seventy-six years old, went to see Hitler and returned repeating Hitler's assertions that he desired peace and wished only to right the wrongs of the Treaty of Versailles. This was a widely held view in Britain and in the United States, for many believed, misunderstanding history, that the Treaty of Versailles represented the height of iniquity, and that for this reason much had to be forgiven the Germans.

During the next two Labour governments, that of 1929 and that of 1945, I came to England frequently as a visitor. Both Labour governments confirmed the typically English democratic method of carrying through a profound economic and social revolution without any great to-do and with scrupulous fairness. The Labour government of 1945 proved equal to the great Liberal administrations of 1868 and 1905, but in keeping with the times its reforms went much farther, even though, in a sense, it only broadened paths pursued by its predecessors. Its Secretary for Foreign Affairs, Ernest Bevin, an old trade unionist, recognized and opposed the danger of Communist aspirations long before the United States did. The two great developments in Europe after 1945—the growth of the welfare state and the liquidation of imperialism—were begun by Britain and then followed less skillfully by continental Europe, at least by that part of Europe which was not subject to fascism or communism. In England itself the democratic process showed its strength again when the voters, in October, 1951, entrusted the continuation of the Labour reform program to Conservative leadership.

I saw only the beginning of this political development during my original stay in London. Then in the summer of 1925 Yetty and I decided to move to Palestine. After attending the Zionist Congress in Vienna and spending our

vacation in the Dolomites and on the Lido, we embarked
at Trieste for Palestine. I had visited that country before,
in 1923, and I had been deeply impressed by its beauty
and by the biblical tone of the life of its people. Now,
in 1925, we arrived there to make our home in Jerusalem.
At that time the city had its center in the historical walled
Old City of Jerusalem, with its Oriental bazaars and its
biblical memories. And what a marvelous city it was,
with new, rapidly growing suburbs outside the walls, and
with its majestic panorama of the barren Judean hills!
From the fertile maritime plain with its citrus groves, the
road ascended steeply to the towering height of the city,
built out of rock, as if in defiance of nature; the descent
was even steeper and more breathtaking toward Jericho
in the subtropical valley, across a magnificent desert landscape.

During our stay in Jerusalem we lived in three different
apartments, all in the neighborhood of the Ratisbonne
monastery. The first one was on the upper floor of a typical Arab house, built with thick stone walls that kept
the high, vaulted rooms cool in summer and warm in
winter. It had no kitchen, bathroom, running water, toilet,
heating, electricity, or telephone; small oil stoves helped in
some respects, but when the cisterns ran dry, water had
to be bought from water carriers. Things became more
complicated after the birth of our son Immanuel on December 6, 1926. Though we loved the coolness of the
apartment, we decided to move to a newly built Arab
house where there were modern conveniences.

Conditions improved rapidly in Palestine in the decade
between 1923 and 1933. The British government built
good roads, the postal service and the telephone were
modernized, and Jerusalem's water supply was improved.

By 1933, life in Jerusalem had become quite comfortable; at the same time the Old City, unchanged in many ways, provided the historical and spiritual link with a great past.

Palestine in my time had all the fascination of the mysterious East. Jerusalem was the holy city of three faiths, an international city, where Jews could preserve the folklore and social habits of their native lands and traditions—European or Oriental, Reform or Orthodox—and mingle with Arab *effendis* and *fellaheen*, with Bedouins, with Catholic, Orthodox, and Coptic monks, with British officials, with Levantine businessmen, with American missionaries and scholars. Under the protective shield of the British mandate, life went on peacefully and in orderly fashion—at least on the surface. The British administration tried to quiet the fears of the large Arab majority that the Zionists might deprive them of their fields and houses. The first British High Commissioner in Palestine, Sir Herbert Samuel, himself a Zionist, had declared officially on June 3, 1921: "Let me, in the first instance, refer once more to the unhappy misunderstanding that has existed with reference to the phrase in the Balfour Declaration 'the establishment in Palestine of a National Home for the Jewish people.' I hear it said in many quarters that the Arab population of Palestine will never agree to their country, their Holy Places, and their lands being taken from them and given to strangers: that they will never agree to a Jewish Government being set up to rule over the Moslem and Christian majority. People say that they cannot understand how it is that the British Government, which is famous throughout the world for its justice, could ever have consented to such a policy. I answer that the British Government, which does, indeed, care for justice above all things, has never consented and will never consent to such a policy. That is not the meaning of the Balfour Declaration. . . . They [the words] mean that the Jews, a people who are scattered throughout the world, but whose hearts are always turned to Palestine, should be enabled to find their home, and that some among them, within the limits that are fixed by the numbers and interests of the present population, should come to Palestine in order to help by their resources and efforts to develop the country to the advantage of all its inhabitants. If any measures are needed to convince the Moslem and Christian population . . . that their rights are really safe, such measures will be taken. For the British Government, the trustee under the Mandate for the happiness of the people of Palestine, would never impose upon them a policy which that people had reason to think was contrary to their religious, their political, and their economic interests."

In my Bohemian homeland, it was not the Austrian government that had made the building of a peaceful multiethnic state impossible, but the spirit of extreme nationalism among its peoples. The case in Palestine was similar. The situation struck me as tragic. The Balfour Declaration of the British Government in November, 1917, had raised high expectations among the Zionists. To the Jews, especially the masses of Eastern Europe, Palestine was the Jewish homeland, *Eretz Israel,* the object of their dreams and longings, the refuge of their souls for two thousand years, a land where history had stood still. At long last, the Diaspora was to end, the curse was to be removed from the Jewish people, the "salvation" awaited by so many generations was to begin.

Unfortunately, certain facts had barely penetrated Jewish consciousness: that the country was not altogether a barren desert, that the Arabs had been living there for

thirteen centuries—a period as long, perhaps, as that of
the Jews dwelling in the land—and that these Arabs
formed a single nation with the surrounding peoples.
Finally, standing at the gates of their country after two
thousand years' migration, Jews were genuinely amazed
and understandably indignant suddenly to find it occupied
by aliens who disputed their right to it. Some of the
Zionist leaders themselves had no idea of the changed
realities in the East. Theodor Herzl, without thinking
primarily of Palestine, had demanded an unpeopled land
for a landless people. And now, at the very moment of
its apparent success, when its boldest hopes seemed about
to be realized, the Zionist movement was confronted with
the fact that Palestine was not an unpeopled land. Further,
it was just at that time that the national consciousness of
the Arabs was awakening. Like many other peoples, the
Arabs, too, were undergoing a process of profound
change. The First World War had stirred them deeply,
and to them, as to the Zionists, the promises of the Great
Powers had offered the vision of a new and glorious life,
a revival of their national culture and political greatness.

Perhaps my study of nationalism in the East better
equipped me to see both sides of the problem. "While the
Zionists pointed out their unique situation," I wrote in
1930, "and the ties of destiny and sentiment which bound
the Jewish people to Palestine, the Arabs, on the other
hand, declared that they would resist, as every other
people would, being turned into a minority in their own
country by immigration from without. They pointed out
that in the Balfour Declaration England had promised
something to the Zionists that did not belong to her."

And now, in fact, the Arab population of Palestine
demanded the self-determination that the Allies had pro-

claimed as one of their war aims; they further insisted on
the introduction of a democratic constitution and the right
to determine how far Jewish immigration was compatible
with Arab rights. To the Arabs, the country seemed too
small to admit large numbers of immigrants without en-
dangering the status of the Arab population, especially the
peasantry. They insisted that the land must remain Arab
in character and culture; Palestine must be reunited with
Syria and with the rest of Arabia, from which it had
been detached solely in the interests of "imperialist
policy." Zionism appeared to the Arabs as an accomplice
of British imperialism; and some Zionist leaders had, indeed, stressed the advantage to the English of a strong
Jewish national home that would counteract Arab national aspirations and thereby guard the road to India.
Zionism, it was said, introduced an element of unrest and
strife into the Middle East, for it seemed certain that the
Arabs would not allow Palestine to become a Jewish
homeland without a bitter struggle. British assurances
about safeguarding Arab rights were regarded by the Arabs
as worthless in face of the financial, organizational, and
propaganda resources of the Zionists throughout the
world. It was regarded as inevitable that poverty would
compel many Arabs to sell their land, and so, in spite
of British assurances, the Arabs feared that Jewish immigration, protected by the British, would create a Jewish
majority and thus lead to a Jewish commonwealth in
Palestine. This, then, was the Arab view in 1930. It
found its outward expression in a number of revolts.
This struggle for independence and political rights was
suppressed by superior military power.

Thus the British Government in Palestine found itself
confronted with a situation that would inevitably lead to

dangerous political tensions. Zionists and Arabs alike
were inextricably involved; the one concentrated on creating, the other on preserving, the basic conditions they
regarded as vital to the very existence of their peoples. It
was a struggle for land and nation, and the viewpoint
of the two peoples has not changed in the decades since.
It has rather grown in determination and bitterness. The
Arab movement owed its growth precisely to the challenge of the Jewish nationalist movement, and it gained
its momentum in resisting Zionist efforts at expansion.
The British administration was caught in the middle of
two conflicting forces which it had helped to create.

The Zionists demanded that the British Government
adhere to the terms of the mandate and support them
actively in increasing Jewish immigration and in expanding Jewish settlements to achieve a Jewish majority in
Palestine, both in population and land ownership. The
Arabs, on the other hand, appealed to the right of self-
determination of the peoples, and to the text of Article
XXII of the League of Nations Covenant; they demanded
the creation of a national government of all the inhabitants
of Palestine in accordance with democratic principles, as
well as the annulment of the Balfour Declaration and the
union of Palestine with the other Arab countries.

Looking back, the fears of the Arabs seemed at the
time largely unjustified. Their majority seemed assured.
From 1919 to the end of 1931, Jewish immigration was
very small. The large majority of European Jewry showed
no inclination to leave their homelands. The Jewish population, by immigration and natural increase, had grown
on the average by only about 10,000 a year, whereas
the Arab population, in the same period, had increased
through its high birthrate by about 20,000 annually. With-

out the triumph of National Socialism in Europe and
without World War II, there was some hope that a bi-
ethnic and multireligious Palestine might have developed,
built on mutual cooperation, which could have taken its
place in the rapidly changing Middle East and become a
force for progress and peace in the whole region. But
the rise of Hitlerism darkened the prospects of a peaceful
and rational settlement in Palestine as in many other
lands. Hitler rejected the idea of the Jews' assimilation
in their own European homelands, and he pursued with
insane fury his goal of making Europe *"Judenrein."* World
War II itself exacerbated the fears of many European
Jews, who saw Hitlerism not as a unique phenomenon
rooted in peculiar German conditions, but as an episode
in the "eternal" war of the Gentiles against the Jews. At
the same time, the Arabs began to fear that the Christian
nations would gladly atone for the crimes of their German
fellow Christians at the expense of the Arabs. Events
after World War II confirmed the fears the Arabs had
voiced twenty years before.

When, after the suppression of the Arab uprising of
1929, I decided to leave the Zionist movement, the decision was not easy. It meant parting with an aspiration
which I had shared for almost twenty years. We had to look
for a new homeland and for a new economic basis for our
existence. We loved Palestine and Jerusalem and we had
many good friends there. Some of them shared my appre-
hensions about the future. I wrote articles for the excellent
Hebrew weekly *Hapoel Hatsair* and helped found an association for Arab-Jewish understanding called *Brith Shalom*
(Covenant of Peace). The Jewish community was still
fairly small; people knew each other, and life was simple,
which we found altogether pleasant. There were no lux-

uries and few people were preoccupied with making
money. Hardly anyone we knew had come to escape
persecution or to improve his economic situation. Rather,
they had come out of what might be called "idealism,"
for want of a better word. There were many brilliant and
remarkable men and women among them. For a community its size, cultural life among the Jews in Jerusalem
was of great intensity and creativity.

The six years I spent in Palestine were productive ones
for me, too. I finished my four books on the Middle East
and on the process of the modernization of non-Western
lands, as well as my book on Martin Buber. The latter
was an intellectual biography of the first fifty years of
Buber's life, based on many documents since lost or inaccessible. Beyond that, it was an attempt to discuss the
intellectual and spiritual problems and influences of a
period (1880-1930) in Central European history that had
conditioned the background of the generation that grew
to maturity in the first decades of this century. The book
soon disappeared from the market, due to the conditions
in Germany; thirty years later it was republished, unchanged but brought up to date in a long final chapter
by my friend Robert Weltsch, who discussed Buber's
work from 1930 to 1960. I welcomed its reappearance,
for it had meant much in my life. In it I tried to sum up,
and to bid farewell to, my own youth. A new chapter in
my life, another encounter with unfamiliar places, people,
and new aspects of history was to begin.

XIII

YEARS OF TRANSITION

I WAS THIRTY-EIGHT when I decided, in the fall of 1929, to seek a new home; I was forty-two when I left Palestine for the United States in the fall of 1933. The years in between were interesting but difficult ones. We kept our residence in Jerusalem, though we were away much of the time. I traveled a great deal in Europe, where I earned part of my living by lecturing. I was Middle East correspondent for the *Frankfurter Zeitung*, the great German liberal newspaper, comparable to the Manchester *Guardian*, and for the *Neue Zürcher Zeitung*, the leading Swiss daily. I established a lasting friendship with the men who at that time ran the Zurich paper, particularly Willy Bretscher, its brilliant editor in chief, who was to become a courageous defender of Western liberty in the crucial years after 1933 when so many Europeans turned away from the heritage of the Enlightenment to an outmoded authoritarianism. His task was especially difficult during the years from 1940 to 1944, when Switzerland was a democratic enclave surrounded on all sides by fascist powers and by traditionalists like Pétain who rejected modern Western civilization. In Switzerland, too, many "democrats" were pusillanimous. They expected the victory of National Socialism and saw, in Mussolini and Pétain, guardians of religion and of "order" in the struggle against communism. These Swiss demanded extreme caution and strictest neutrality; they did not prevail, however. The *Neue Zürcher Zeitung* remained an outspoken enemy of fascism and adhered to its faith in the ultimate victory of the democracies. Its steadfast courage during Europe's darkest hour was the finest hour of the *Neue Zürcher Zeitung*. Hans Barth, then an editor on the paper, wrote the most probing and trenchant analysis of the German scholars who had helped to defeat democracy and the "West" in Germany. Barth later became professor of philosophy at Zurich University, and whenever I came to Zurich in the years after World War II, an event I always looked forward to, I enjoyed the hospitality of Barth and his wife in their lovely home high above the Lake of Zurich.

Switzerland and Great Britain have been my favorite European nations for many years. Wordsworth stressed the similarity of the two nations:

> Two voices are there; one is of the sea,
> One of the mountains; each a mighty voice.
> In both from age to age thou didst rejoice,
> They were thy chosen music, Liberty!

Both countries have set an example of an affirmative nationalism that emphasizes cohesive collective power, and yet is compatible with the preservation of individual liberty and a nonmilitaristic society. During the age of the Enlightenment, in Western Europe and in North America, nationalism began as a movement whose goal was the assertion of individual rights against state absolutism; it was a liberal, humanitarian movement in an ever-widening, open society. Britain and Switzerland, the territorial nation-state based on equal rights for all, provided an opportunity for various ethnic groups to live together in peaceful coexistence. By contrast, in most of Europe, after the abortive revolution of 1848, nationalism increasingly began to stress the exclusiveness of various ethnic and linguistic groups and to arouse their pride of race. German and Italian nationalists claimed that all people of German or Italian descent must form part of one great German or Italian nation-state. Nationalist passions were aroused to fight to "redeem" peoples of their race who were not yet included in the nation-state to which, it was asserted, they belonged ethnically. In a darkening European world of violence and fanaticism, these nationalist passions were often the force that undermined democracy and corrupted a people's humanitarian spirit. I had witnessed such developments in Bohemia and in Palestine. Switzerland with its various ethnic, linguistic, and religious populations had followed a different path.

In December, 1938, at the very hour when nationalism based on an assertion of common descent and ancestry as the chief criteria seemed about to triumph in Europe, the Swiss Federal Council, in a message on "the meaning and mission of Switzerland," rejected the concept of race or common descent as the basis of a state and as the factor determining political and cultural allegiance. "The Swiss national idea," the message read, "is not based upon race or biological factors, it rests on a spiritual decision. . . . The Swiss Federal State is an association of free republics; it does not swallow them, it federates them. The cantonal republics maintain their individuality, and thereby they are the sources and pillars of our intellectual wealth, the strongest bulwark against intellectual uniformity. Next to federalism and democracy, Switzerland is based upon respect for the dignity of the individual. The respect for the right and liberty of the human personality is so deeply anchored in the Swiss idea that we can regard it as its basic concept, and can proclaim its defense as an essential task of the nation. We recognize the individual human personality as the strongest creative force in the life of the spirit, and the state has accordingly limited its own sphere of power."

During the early years of the 1930's, as the crisis brought about by nationalism deepened, I traveled widely in Europe and in the Middle East. As a Middle Eastern correspondent, I had the opportunity of prolonged visits to many countries, from Egypt to Iraq. At the time, Egypt was by far the most important country in the Middle East and the focal point of the changing trends of the time. And so it is again today. Even in Baghdad, however, one could witness astonishing transformations. I met Mohammed Fadhil Jamali, then a young man, son of an orthodox Shiite theologian in the holy city of Kadhimain, a medieval, traditionalist setting. After studying at the American University of Beirut, he received his doctorate at Teachers College, Columbia University. He became betrothed to an American, Sarah Hayden Powell, and was conversant with contemporary English and American literature and politics. He later played an important role in the Iraqi government before the overthrow of the monarchy.

Life in 1931 brought many gifts. I spent an unforgettably lovely winter and spring in Egypt. Then in May, I rejoined my family in Germany, and during the summer of

1931, I visited the Soviet Union for the *Frankfurter Zeitung*, to study the nationality problem there. That summer was an extremely hot one, and it was practically impossible to escape the sweltering heat. There was no ice in Moscow, and food was scarce and tasteless. It was probably the lowest period in Soviet history, as regards the amenities of life, which had become indescribably drab. Yet the Russian people and the Russian land exercised their attraction upon me.

During my Russian stay I was neither shadowed nor observed, except perhaps by the hotel personnel. The Stalinist police state had not yet reached the insanity of the later period of the purges. The nationalities were still allowed some of the linguistic and cultural freedom they had gained under Lenin. I was allowed to travel wherever I wished, and since I then spoke Russian more fluently than I do now, I could have held unhindered conversations with all kinds of people. However, a certain reserve or shyness has always kept me from interviewing great men or the common man and from following the methods introduced by modern journalism. Yet I found everyone, including the militia, exceedingly helpful and polite to foreigners. Nevertheless, the atmosphere of general distrust and indoctrination was so pervasive that no visitor who knew Russian and felt sympathy for the people could escape it. Poland was then certainly neither a democracy nor a model of Western civilization, yet when I reached the small Polish frontier town on my return trip, I felt I was again breathing free air.

After leaving Moscow, I visited Leningrad, the Ukraine, and the Crimea. On the train from Moscow to Simferopol I shared my compartment with a small, gracious, elderly lady, who to my surprise introduced herself as Olga Knipper, the actress whom Chekhov had married in 1901, three years before his death. In 1931 Chekhov himself would have been only seventy-one years old—my own age as I write these lines—and yet Chekhov and his world seemed so far away, so irretrievably lost.

In the Crimea (then an autonomous Tartar Soviet Republic) I visited the beautiful Russian Riviera, the Tartar towns, and the Jewish agricultural settlements of the Agro-Joint, an American philanthropical institution. Leningrad made the greatest impression on me of any Russian city. I found it much more pleasant, beautiful, and civilized than Moscow. I could not imagine anyone liking Moscow, at least in 1931, but I could easily understand why people fell in love with Leningrad even in 1931.

This was my last visit to Russia. The three decades since then have wrought great changes in Russia as they did elsewhere. Here, too, continuity and change interact. Some time I would like to see Russia again, to visit Leningrad and Moscow, Samarkand and Irkutsk. But the year in which I saw Russia for the last time was also the year in which I "discovered" America. I went there in the search for a home and for a secure livelihood.

Thus in the early fall of 1931 I sailed for the United States on one of the large ships of the North German Lloyd Line. It was not a propitious time to look for a permanent job. The Great Depression in Europe and in the United States was then at its height. But I had set my heart on going to the United States, for I was convinced that with its open, pluralistic society it promised a greater measure of freedom and diversity than was possible in Europe. I hoped to find a teaching position where I could try to fulfill my vocation as a teacher, a vocation which I had discovered earlier in Siberia, lecturing to my fellow prisoners.

Ultimately I was not disappointed in either of my expectations. I undertook two exploratory trips, in 1931 and in 1933, under the auspices of the Institute of International Education. I owed this support to the recommendation of the Chancellor of the Hebrew University in Jerusalem, Judah L. Magnes, an American who shared my deep anxiety about the future of Arab-Jewish relations in Palestine. The Institute, then a small organization, headed by Dr. Duggan and Edward R. Murrow, arranged lectures for me in midwestern and eastern colleges. I gave my first lecture at Macalester College in Minnesota, and then I worked my way slowly eastward, speaking at many small colleges in Ohio and Illinois.

It was my first contact with the vastness of the United States, with the friendliness of its people, with the diversity of its landscapes and mores. It was the aspect of diversity more than that of uniformity—and both exist side by side —which impressed me on my first trips.

When I arrived in the United States, in 1931, Herbert Hoover was President. My second visit, from late September, 1933, to early February, 1934, coincided with the beginning of President Franklin D. Roosevelt's administration, with a new era in American history, the era of the welfare state. I was lunching at a New York restaurant when Prohibition ended in November, 1933; two months later, in a Des Moines hotel lobby, I listened to the first nationwide broadcast of a Metropolitan Opera performance. Both were noteworthy dates in the social and intellectual history of the United States.

The Great Depression of the 1930's was a time of trial that will not be forgotten by those who lived through it.

The generation that has grown up since the Second World War can hardly imagine what it was like. Yet the Depression left a better America—a less strident and self-confident America, a nation with an aroused social conscience and a deeper awareness of cultural and spiritual values. Unfortunately, much of the lesson of the Great Depression has since been lost amid the prosperity of the present postwar period. I observed one enduring result of America's new cultural awareness as I toured state universities and colleges throughout the country: their campuses had been improved by new buildings erected with public funds. These public works during the Depression went far toward transforming the face of academe.

In the fall of 1933 I lectured for six weeks at the country's leading center of advanced adult education, the New School for Social Research in New York City, located in Greenwich Village. I have always found it stimulating to lecture before adult audiences. In discussing history and human attitudes with them, I can refer to their own experiences and to their knowledge of the past. The lecturer has to be at his best with such audiences. Students in university classes form a captive audience; they have to attend and study in order to receive their degree. But adults usually hold down a job during the day and often carry the burdens of family responsibility, so they will come to their evening classes only if they find them truly worthwhile.

As it turned out, I was to lecture at the New School for the next thirty years. After I settled in New England in 1934, these lectures gave me the opportunity to come to New York every week and to remain in touch with my many friends there. Among them I will mention only two: Clara W. Mayer, one of the early pillars of the school, its

dean for a very long time and in many ways its "soul"; and
the American historian Koppel S. Pinson, who shared my
interest in the history of nationalism and of Germany, and
whose broad humanity and fairness I much admired. He
was one of those considerate, friendly, and understanding
scholars who form the strength of American academic life.

In October, 1933, William Allan Neilson, president of
Smith College, attended two of my classes at the New
School. This remarkable man was then looking for some-
one to fill the chair of Professor Sidney B. Fay, who had
gone to Harvard, and though I was a newcomer to the
academic profession, Neilson had the courage to invite me
to join the faculty as Professor of Modern European
History in the fall of 1934. Before doing so, I visited the
Smith campus twice to lecture there and to be introduced
to the faculty and the student body.

Between my visits to Northampton I spent five weeks in
Des Moines, Iowa, where the Carnegie Foundation was
conducting an experiment in intensive adult education on
world affairs. I lectured five evenings a week to groups
meeting in the local high schools. Today, it is almost impossible to recall the difficulties we encountered at the time
in discussing international relations. The 1930's had
brought the economic depression while war clouds were
gathering over Asia and Europe. With these events, the
isolationist attitude in the United States hardened. In
April, 1934, Hiram W. Johnson, the veteran Senator from
California, sponsored the Debt-Default Act, which banned
transactions in the securities of governments that had de-
faulted on their American war debts; this bill also pro-
hibited Americans from making private loans to these
governments. In the following year, American neutrality
legislation was passed by Congress. It was inspired by

Senator Gerald P. Nye's hearings before the Special Committee Investigating the Munitions Industry. These hearings intensified American complacency and strengthened the conviction that the United States' resolute will to peace and its fortunate geographic position guaranteed its security. Senator Nye fervently believed that the evil machinations of British imperialism and the armament manufacturers' greed for profits had forced America into the First World War, and most Americans shared his over-simplified views. Was it not best to abandon the "so-called democracies," Great Britain and France, to their fate? Even President Roosevelt in the beginning was an isolationist who shared his people's prejudices regarding Europe's ever-recurrent imperialist conflicts and their naïve faith in America's innocence of such involvement. Under these conditions, it was not too difficult for Communist and pro-fascist spokesmen to gain the ear of the American public, especially of its youth. Did not the energetic "young" nations—for some mysterious reason Germany and Italy regarded themselves as "young"—represent the wave of the future as against the "decadent" democracies? Were not the "have-nots"—and Germany setting out to conquer Europe was regarded as a "have-not"—entitled to find their place in the sun?

Yet the attempt to dispel this attitude was an exhilarating experience for a newcomer who was touched by the unfailing friendliness of his audiences despite the wide divergence between their opinions and his. In that respect I shall long remember the critical year of 1940 and the ten weeks I spent then at the summer school of the University of Colorado in Boulder. The debate on isolationism, aid to the Allies, and compulsory military service was at its height. The Communists and fellow travelers, with their usual shrewd polemics and air of superiority, advocated neutrality, took an openly anti-British and pro-German slant. The party line had come full circle from its violent anti-fascist phase in August, 1939; in June, 1941, it would swing, just as suddenly and as strongly, to anti-fascism. Though there were few Communists on the Boulder campus, their arguments and seeming historical knowledge reinforced the prevailing isolationism and anti-British feeling with "scholarly" rationalization. Besides my regular courses, I gave public lectures on the international situation twice a week in the handsome auditorium of the new theater building on the campus. It was a long time before the initial hostility to my views gave way to a willingness to at least ponder my arguments.

XIV

AMERICAN INSTITUTIONS OF LEARNING

In THE FALL OF 1934 I began teaching at Smith College. I was to remain there for the next fifteen years. I started this new career late in life, and I suffered in this, as I have at other times, from the fact that most things have come to me late, perhaps too late, in life. Yet I was fortunate to find my first teaching position at Smith College. Smith is located in Northampton, in western Massachusetts, my favorite part of the United States. New England's countryside is lovely and endlessly varied. Except in the large cities, the traditions of the past live on quietly and unobtrusively without stultifying the present, as they so often do in Europe. No part in the United States reminds one so strongly of England, and no part of the United States is at the same time more American than New England.

A small town like Northampton has a better public library than many large European cities, and the library, endowed largely by local people, plays a much more important part in the life of the town. Schools in the United States may not be better than those in Europe, but, being run by boards of education composed of local residents, they command much greater public support and a feeling of responsibility for curriculum and teachers. As far as my memory goes, European children generally disliked or feared school. American children on the whole are fond of their schools. There is less provincialism in small New England towns than in similar cities in Europe. The difference is due partly to the fact that New England women are generally more open-minded, better informed, and more socially conscious than their counterparts in Europe. I found the people of New England invariably friendly and ready to help in every way they could, though at the same time they respected privacy and were careful not to interfere. Probably this trait is even more evident in a college community.

Throughout its history, the United States has exercised a strong assimilative power upon the children of immigrants. We saw this process at work in our son, Immanuel, who was seven years old when we came to the States. Immanuel was educated entirely in New England—first at the Smith College Day School, then at Williston Junior School in neighboring Easthampton, and for the next four years at Deerfield Academy, which has become one of the leading preparatory schools in the country under the inspired leadership of Mr. and Mrs. Frank L. Boyden. After that he entered Harvard, and after time out to serve in World War II, was graduated summa cum laude in political science in 1949. In the same year his future wife, Vera Sharpe, whom he had met in Paris in 1948, graduated from Mount Holyoke College. They spent the following year in Europe, she studying international law and organization in Geneva, he on a Sheldon Travelling Fellowship. On their return in 1950 they were married, and he attended Yale Law School, from which he graduated cum laude in 1953. In the years since he has been a corporation lawyer, and is now a partner in one of the large law firms in downtown New York.

The European immigrant is struck by the freedom, the informality, and the mobility of life in the United States. In Northampton one hardly noticed that there was a police force. The newcomer did not have to register with them or report his address or change of domicile. In America, although social stratification exists, it is unobtrusive. The academic profession is free of the *Standesdünkel,* the caste spirit of superiority, which I remember from my days in Europe. There is no Herr Professor, much less a Frau Professor. Recently I read an interesting story by an anthropologist, Oscar Lewis, called *The Children of San-chez, the Autobiography of a Mexican Family.* It tells of Manuel, a Mexican migrant worker who comes to California and lives there under very difficult conditions. Yet in his simple way he gives a moving account of the social mobility and freedom in the United States, so very different from the conditions in Mexico. A similar contrast could be made, though to a lesser degree, with Western European life.

Northampton is situated in the Connecticut River valley, but a short ride brings one into the Berkshire Hills, with their picturesque trails, forests and lakes, and hill towns like Cummington. Not far distant is the town of Lenox, with its wide expanse of meadows and woods. Hawthorne wrote *The House of the Seven Gables* and his *Tanglewood Tales* in this glorious spot. Now Tanglewood, at Lenox, is the site of the annual summer festivals of the Boston Symphony Orchestra, which were started under the direction of the late Serge Koussevitzky. My wife and I were frequent visitors at the Tanglewood concerts during their first seasons, before they became popular and crowded. My wife learned how to drive and from 1938 to 1956 we owned a car. All during my fifteen years at Smith we explored New England, from the hills and mountains of the west and north to the Atlantic shore at Cape Cod and in Maine. The beauty of the landscape is matched by the beauty of many small New England towns themselves, with their graceful, simple churches and elegant church spires, their impressive village green and neat white frame houses.

American institutions of higher education differ from those in Europe in several respects. The courses of study here are more rigorous and students are more conscientious. Just as in Europe, students enter college after twelve years of primary and secondary schooling, but they are not so well prepared as students of the Central European gymnasiums or the French lycées. Until quite recently, university students in Europe represented a small minority of a nation's youth and came almost exclusively from the privileged classes. In the United States, however, a much larger percentage of the sons or daughters of workers, farmers, and immigrants enter college; many come from mediocre or inferior high schools, but the colleges do an excellent job in weeding out noncollege material in the freshman and sophomore years. When American students reach the junior year at the better colleges, they are the equal of most students in European universities. I think it is fortunate that the purely professional training is left to the postgraduate schools in the States. Thus one's education here may last several years longer than in Europe, but the student receives a firmer grounding in what may be called *studium generale*, the broad substructure of

liberal arts, of political, cultural, and scientific understanding. The universities in Europe are state sponsored and
therefore resemble each other closely. American colleges
and universities are much more varied; each has its distinctive character.

In American universities a close personal contact exists
between teacher and student. A similar give-and-take spirit
is rarely found in Europe, where the professor remains at
a distance, an unapproachable figure inaccessible to even
his younger colleagues, who rarely dare to contradict him.
When European students seek guidance, they generally
receive it from young teaching assistants, and even their
number and their time are limited. In the United States, by
contrast, a professor who takes his task seriously is always
accessible to his students.

Students came often to tea at our house near the
college, on Dryads Green. (The enchanting name of this
quiet street was fully deserved; it was shadowed by old
trees in which squirrels rather than dryads made their
home.) Our house was near a steep ravine of almost
impenetrable brush and undergrowth through which the
Mill River—in spite of its name, a typical rural brook—
flowed into Paradise Pond. One afternoon and one evening
in the week were given over to discussing personal and
world problems with my students. My wife tried to create
for the young people living away from their families the
atmosphere of a home. The steady contact with the world
of scholarship and cultural heritage, on the one hand, and
with young people ever questing for knowledge, on the
other, is the real reward of the university teacher.

Until very recently American professors were underpaid
as compared with other professions. But the leisure for
intellectual pursuits, for studying and writing, and the con-

stant contact with youth—these opportunities compensated for the meager salaries. Although small college towns are fairly provincial, campuses generate their own intellectual and cultural life, and so such towns really offer more in music, lectures, and theaters than many larger cities. And since American society is addicted to the quest for wealth, pleasure, and comfort, faculty life also affords a privileged existence by being in this respect "un-American," in setting an example of "high thinking" and "low living." In an affluent society there is greater need than ever for some to stress the more enduring intellectual or spiritual values of our civilization.

Because I entered a teaching career twenty years later than the average instructor, I taught advanced and graduate students, not freshmen or sophomores. I never taught basic required courses, only electives. Thus I had a student body truly interested in my course, and I taught only subjects that vitally interested me. I never used textbooks; wherever possible, the supplementary reading came from the original sources. Every year I varied the details of selection and presentation so as not to allow the courses to become stale. I was able to introduce two new courses into the curriculum. One dealt with the social, intellectual, and political transformation of Asia and North Africa in the late nineteenth and early twentieth centuries under the impact of modern imperialism. Today, of course, this is an accepted part of a college curriculum, but in 1934 few students knew much about modern developments in Turkey, Egypt, India, or China. The other course dealt with the intellectual history of Europe, from Rousseau and Goethe to Nietzsche and Ibsen. I omitted English thought because most students were familiar with its literature, and time was limited. In the 1930's most history courses emphasized political and economic developments, diplomacy, and political institutions; since then more attention has been paid to the history of ideas—both European and American. After World War II, I replaced my course on imperialism with a course on the history of nationalism, stressing the variety of national traditions. Throughout my years as a teacher I experienced the truth of the old saying, that *homines dum docent discunt* (men learn while teaching). My own progress was perhaps reflected in my writings on the nature and history of nationalism and the history and impact of ideas.

The president of an American college sets the tone of its academic and social life to a large degree. William Allan Neilson was one of the greatest men I have met. He was raised in the poverty and piety of a Calvinist home in Scotland and had preserved the homely virtues of this background. Although he abandoned the Calvinist faith, he could still recite from memory great parts of the Bible many years afterward. He was a scholar and educator—he had been Professor of English Literature at Bryn Mawr and Harvard—and at the same time an excellent administrator, knowledgeable about details, budget-minded, and yet daring and open to innovations. Above all he was deeply human, interested in the individual teacher and student, always helpful and wise. He was gifted with a quick sense of humor, and his speeches reflected his broadminded tolerance and his wide interests.

Neilson came to Smith from Harvard in 1917, and was the first layman to become president of the college (his predecessors were ordained New England ministers). He guided the transition of the college from an old-fashioned, "Victorian" institution to a modern school of the first rank, where young women of the mid-twentieth century were given a broad international outlook and a sense of commitment. Smith College was one of the first institutions to introduce a "junior year abroad" (in Paris, Florence, Munich, and Madrid) and to stress the study of continental European civilizations. (Asian and African studies entered the curriculum only after Neilson's retirement in 1939.)

Under Neilson's guidance, the intellectual and artistic life of the college community was an exciting one. The Music Department counted many distinguished members; the homes of the two resident composers, Werner Josten and Frederic Jacobi, were gracious settings for musical performances. At Smith one met famous men and women from all over the country, and many foreign scholars and lecturers who came to the United States and visited the campus. There was no provincialism in the college atmosphere. Neilson constantly invited foreign scholars to join the faculty as permanent members.

Thus I became friends with Kurt Koffka, the German Gestalt psychologist; Giuseppe Antonio Borgese, the Italian literary historian and critic; and Alfred Einstein, the great German musicologist. Einstein and Koffka were brilliant scholars and at the same time men of wide culture. Einstein impressed me as a model scholar endowed with the great gift of personal simplicity and charm. Borgese had an artistic temperament—a colorful personality, brilliant and volatile, as unmistakably Italian as the historian Gaetano Salvemini, who frequently visited Smith College. Borgese was also passionately involved in contemporary political events. Before he was thirty, he had published a novel, *Rubé*, which had slight literary value but which was truly representative of the troubled European mind of the period (1921). In 1937 he wrote an important and deeply personal book entitled *Goliath, The March of Fascism*. It was written in a highly individualistic Italianate English and told the reader as much about Borgese as about Mussolini. Yet it was a very valuable study of the Italian roots of fascism. Borgese later left Smith College for the University of Chicago, where he became the leading spirit of the Committee on Europe, which maintained that after Munich the United States could not afford to remain isolated from Europe, since the events of the hour would affect all mankind. The Committee attempted to formulate basic principles for a future society "from which practical applications might be deduced, leaving active statesmen and diplomats to deal with decisions which cannot be postponed and compromises which cannot be avoided."

William Allan Neilson was one of the active members of the Committee on Europe from the beginning. In 1940 its name was changed to the Committee of Fifteen. In addition to Borgese and Neilson, it included, among others, Herbert Agar, Hermann Broch, Van Wyck Brooks, William Yandell Elliott, Thomas Mann, Lewis Mumford, Reinhold Niebuhr, Gaetano Salvemini, and myself. We held a conference in Atlantic City from May 24 through May 26, 1940, during the critical days of the battle for France. A Declaration on World Democracy—"The City of Man"—was drawn up by the conference and published in November, 1940. "In an era of Apocalypse," it proclaimed, "we call for a Millennium." Its spirit and phraseology bore the unmistakable impress of Borgese, yet it expressed the fears and hopes felt by many Americans in the fateful year of 1940.

The Declaration was written in the shadow of the greatest danger ever to threaten the survival of Western civilization. Fascism was on the verge of triumph. Much more than had communism, fascism had rejected everything for which free men stand: its dogma was the permanent degradation of man and its banner was the glorification of war as man's noblest calling.

In 1964, it might be useful to recall the words of the Committee of Fifteen, written in the midst of a war which, like all great wars, could not be won by arms alone:

> "First of all, we reaffirm that the meaning and goal of human life, individual and collective, are progress and growth in intellect and action, and that peace, universal peace, is the prerequisite of progress and growth. . . . The perpetuity of change and struggle need not be identified with the alleged inevitability of slaughter and arson. War, as practiced by man in the short span of time which history records, is neither a biological fate nor a moral law. Far from being the most shining light of life as proclaimed by [fascism], war is chaos and horror. Slavery and human sacrifices also had their apologists and priests; they also were revered as immutable features in the society of man, and were abolished at last. . . . Nothing eternal and holy inheres in the institution of war. Whatever the misuse of a commanding ideal in the ideological verbiage of the gay Twenties, the outlawry of war is and remains the next step in the progress of man."

But, the Declaration warned, just as the price of liberty is eternal vigilance, the price of peace is the readiness to fight. It quoted Walt Whitman, that "it is provided in the very essence of things, that from any fruition of success, no matter what, shall come forth something to make a greater struggle necessary. Each horizon opens into another, and the march from horizon to horizon is long and very difficult and exacting, but it need not and must not be clothed in the degradation and dehumanization involved in war, which on this very account is the ideal of fascism."

My schedule at Smith College started on Monday noon and was over on Wednesday noon. That gave me ample opportunity for research and for teaching and lecturing at other colleges. In the summer of 1938 I taught at the University of California in Berkeley, and we used the opportunity to travel the northern and southern routes across the American continent. We were again very much impressed with the great variety and regional differences in this nation.

I taught at Harvard on many occasions from 1935 to 1958, three times during the regular fall and spring terms and twelve times during summer school. In 1936 I delivered a series of lectures which were published by the Harvard University Press the following year under the title *Force or Reason*. It was my first book written in English and the first to go through four printings. It dealt with the issues of the time, seen in historical perspective, from the point of view of a historian of ideas.

In my seminars at Harvard I met many foreign students and others who have since become important teachers and scholars. With two of them, Karl Deutsch and Peter Viereck, I have kept in touch all these years. In addition to my classes and seminars, I delivered weekly public lectures on the international situation in the critical summers of 1939, 1941, and 1942. These were hot and humid summers, and the New Lecture Hall at Harvard was not air conditioned, yet the events of the time were so exciting that the large hall was always crowded. In the summer of 1939 I shared the platform with Max Lerner.

In those years I was more absorbed with the contemporary scene than I am today. Despite my crowded schedule I also continued my long labor on *The Idea of Nationalism,* using the resources of the excellent Widener Library. Later I used that library for most of my research on my books *Pan-Slavism, American Nationalism,* and *The Mind of Germany.* I am generally happy and content in the atmosphere of libraries anyway, but nowhere have I felt as much at home as at the Widener. I miss it sometimes as much as I miss Harvard's unique atmosphere.

XV

WORLD WAR AND
WORLD REVOLUTION

IN 1944 *The Idea of Nationalism* was
published by Macmillan. It went through many printings
and was translated into several languages. The book is a
study of the development of nationalism and universalism
from ancient times to 1789, the beginning of the great
democratic revolution that was profoundly to change the
Western world. This revolution, which has since spread to
all peoples and continents, originated in the United States
and in France and was the first chapter in the age of equality. Edward Shils has defined this egalitarian revolution as
"an opening up of the creative powers of ordinary people;
it involves an appreciation of their rights and potentialities
as individuals, of their capacities for expression, for happiness, for knowledge." The recognition of the rights of the
common man is the essence of the revolution of our time.
That revolution, of course, is a continuation of the "permanent revolution" which began in Western Europe in the
seventeenth and eighteenth centuries. The greatest challenge to this movement came from fascism, which was a
repudiation of the trend toward equality and modernity.
Fascism, however, was not, as contemporary Marxists

argue, the final stage of capitalism, but rather the last-ditch stand of precapitalist forms of society based upon the inequality of men and peoples.

The transition from premodern to modern society throughout the world is taking place under the aegis of nationalism. In *The Idea of Nationalism* I tried to trace the historical roots of nationalism. I planned this volume as one of a series of volumes to be called "The Age of Nationalism." This series was to distingush the various forms and philosophies which nationalism assumed in the different countries. In view of the spread of nationalism in Europe in the nineteenth century—and throughout the world in our own century—such a study assumes encyclopedic proportions. I have collected a vast amount of material on the subject, aided by the generous assistance of the Institute of Advanced Study at Princeton, where I did research when a member in 1948 and in 1955. But thus far I have not had time to organize these extensive materials, nor have I had the assistance that would allow me the several years of concentration required for this task. However, I have completed a number of studies that comprise large fragments of this projected work: *Prophets and Peoples: Studies in Nineteenth-Century Nationalism* (Macmillan, 1946); *Pan-Slavism, Its History and Ideology* (University of Notre Dame Press, 1953); *Nationalism and Liberty: The Swiss Example* (Macmillan, 1956); *American Nationalism* (Macmillan, 1957); and *The Mind of Germany* (Scribner's, 1960). Finally, I attempted a provisional conclusion in *The Age of Nationalism: The First Era of Global History* (Harper, 1962), a survey of the period from 1789 to 1961, dealing with the various forms and content nationalism assumed in the leading nations of Europe, Asia, Africa, and the Americas, and the dialectic relationship between the universal growth of nationalism and the emergence of an interdependent mankind. Such a study, I thought, might be useful in order to understand our time and the conceptual framework of its theory of politics.

The world revolution set in motion by two global wars has profoundly changed human relationships. Much of my writing and teaching has been aimed at increasing our understanding of this revolution by uncovering its historical roots and analyzing its national and global development. More than one hundred and thirty years ago, De Tocqueville identified this revolution with "the gradual development of the principle of equality." In the introduction to his *Democracy in America*, he recognized this development as "a providential fact." As De Tocqueville saw it, "It has all the chief characteristics of such a fact: it is universal, it is lasting, it constantly eludes all interference, and all events as well as all men contribute to its progress." For this emerging new world, "a new science of politics is needed. This, however, is what we think of least; placed in the middle of a rapid stream, we obstinately fix our eyes on the ruins that may still be described upon the shore we have left, while the current hurries us away." This new science of politics has to be based upon history, not a history imprisoned by the past, but a history that enlightens the present by giving perspective to the revolutions transforming the past.

In the 1920's and 1930's, most of Western Europe and North America refused to acknowledge the revolution that overturned the foundations of traditional European life and as a reaction produced fascism. The misunderstanding was in no way confined to one class or party. In her autobiography *La force de l'âge* (*The Prime of Life*),

Simone de Beauvoir tells us how she and Jean-Paul Sartre lived in Berlin under Hitler, and yet were entirely absorbed in their studies. They did not like the Germans, but they remained unaware of the effect a fascist victory would have on peace and on Europe. The communist interpretation of recent history has tried to persuade us that it was primarily the "Cliveden set," the elite of the British capitalist class, that engendered and welcomed the "appeasement" at Munich. Yet people like Mme. de Beauvoir were delighted with Munich. "I felt not the faintest pang of conscience at my reaction," she writes. "I felt I had escaped death, now and for ever. There was even an element of triumph in my relief. Decidedly, I thought, I was born happy; no misfortune could ever touch me." In 1938, most socialists, capitalists, ardent anti-fascists, and moderate middle-of-the-road democrats in Western Europe felt much the same way. They remembered World War I and wished to preserve peace. Neville Chamberlain was not the only one who believed that Munich represented "peace in our time." Of course, Hitler and many Germans knew otherwise.

The American attitude resembled Western Europe's but lagged behind it. At first many Americans who were concerned with world affairs criticized the "appeasement" policy of Western Europe—often in highly moralistic tones —even though the peace efforts of the British and French leaders had the wide support of their peoples. But when the British abandoned appeasement and declared war in September, 1939, many of these same Americans were seized by an almost panicky desire to stay out of the war. Unlike the situation today, when most Americans seem determined to resist the communist world "conspiracy," in 1939 few Americans were eager to combat the fascist threat. It took the Japanese attack on Pearl Harbor and the German declaration of war to force the United States to abandon this attitude.

To a large extent, such attitudes were a heritage of the American people's failure to understand the real meaning of the events that occurred from 1917 to 1920. After 1918, Germany, Italy, and Spain rejected modern Western civilization; at about the same time, the peoples of Asia began to awaken to an awareness of the modern world and nationalism. These two events were, of course, part of a worldwide revolution and counterrevolution in which the United States was inextricably involved, as were all the democratic nations of the West. Unfortunately, the democracies did not recognize this fact; this failure of mind, not economic factors, was primarily responsible for the decline of the Western democracies after 1918. The economic crisis of the 1930's merely accelerated a process which had begun years before, and the crisis itself was partly engendered by this failure of mind and morality and partly by the growing spirit of materialism and the drive for economic and political autarchy among the Western powers.

After the initial shock of September, 1939, had worn off, small groups throughout the United States formed "Aid to the Allies committees." In Northampton, President Neilson took the initiative. He was helped greatly by the efforts of a former First Lady, the widow of President Calvin Coolidge, who lived in Northampton where her husband had practiced law. Grace Coolidge was an unusually intelligent, highly cultured, and unassuming woman who represented the best of the New England tradition. She led a quiet life, but was well informed on the political and international issues of the day. In 1940, when it demanded courage to speak up, urging all-out aid to Britain,

even at the risk of war, she lent her name and prestige to
the cause without hesitation.

Only a small group of Americans felt that this nation
had a direct stake in the European conflict, and many of
them were themselves of European origin. On the Smith
faculty there were many who were neutral or noncom-
mitted, who saw no reason to "fight Britain's battles."
Later, when Americans were to complain of a similar
neutralist attitude among Asian or African peoples, I
recalled the nonalignment mentality of so many Americans
in the European power struggle of 1939, and the high-
sounding moral reasons which were used to defend it.

After the United States entered the war in 1941, Americans tended to oversimplify the issues. Many believed that
the total defeat of Germany and Japan would solve all the
world's problems, and that Britain and Russia were equally
trustworthy as allies. Some even thought that after the war
we should be on guard against wily British "imperialism"
even more than against Russian expansionist ambitions.
As it turned out, it was the British who first warned
America about Russian intentions. First, Ernest Bevin
asked us to help stop Russia's advance into the Mediterranean; then Winston Churchill warned us of the Communists' real intentions in his memorable speech at Fulton,
Missouri, in March, 1946. Many Americans were still
unmoved, however, and believed that these British statesmen wished to draw us into another war—this time against
communism—for the benefit of British imperialism. The
American reaction was an offer to mediate between Russia
and Britain, interposing the United States as a kind of
"third force."

During those years I did not indulge in a similar distrust
of Britain nor entertain any such illusions about Russia.

With my knowledge of national traditions and ideologies, I distinguished between the two nations. Britain fought Germany without being attacked, while Russia—and the United States—could claim the defense of no great cause other than that of self-defense. Britain was the heartland of that Western liberty which the fascist powers contemptuously rejected. Russia under the tsars and Soviets alike had neither honored nor practiced this liberty. *The New Leader*, a weekly published in New York by S. M. Levitas, a dedicated Socialist of Russian Menshevik background, referred in every issue to this fundamental distinction between British democracy and Russian communism. At a time when this distinction was blurred by official and grass-roots American opinion, such an attitude demanded courage. It was a comfort to me, in those years, to be able to discuss the world situation with Levitas.

In the 1960's, as in the 1930's, misinterpretations of the past haunt many people and cause them to draw over-simplified conclusions. Many Americans again believe that an all-out "victory" over communism would solve all our problems. This time it is not the memory of the Peace of Versailles but that of Munich which dominates their minds, with Khrushchev playing the role of Hitler and the gnawing fear that we might play the role of Neville Chamberlain. But the two situations are different. Khrushchev is not Hitler (nor, of course, do West Germany's policies bear any resemblance to Hitler's policies, despite the allegations of Communist propaganda); Russia's whole history and national tradition is different from that of modern Germany; above all, the West of the 1960's is not the West of 1938. The democratic West—the United States, France, and Britain—was then disunited and Britain and the United States were disarmed. It did not understand the need of concerted action and armed vigilance; it did not really understand the nature of fascism and totalitarianism. Today, the West is wide awake to the Communist challenge, and is, with the exception of De Gaulle's France, cooperating and armed as never before. In the 1930's, the West was in the grip of an unprecedented economic depression; in the 1960's, it is more affluent than at any time in its history. Russia's economic and military power is not growing in proportion to that of the West; everywhere communism is beset with grave problems, internal dissensions, agricultural failures, the lack of sufficient capital and skilled manpower, the inability to make any headway in free Europe (far different from the devastated Europe of 1946 when the Communist parties were riding high in Italy and France). Russia is likewise making little progress in Asia or Africa: countries like India, Iraq, Egypt, Guinea, and the Congo, which once seemed propitious soil for Communist expansion, for various reasons, in recent years have shown a single-minded dedication to their nationalist self-interests. Despite all this, some Americans still believe in the myth that communism is "gaining" on us and that it represents a monolithic international conspiracy—the Sino-Soviet split notwithstanding.

There can be no doubt that the West's position today is far different from that of the 1930's. Likewise, there is a vast difference between the Germany of the 1930's and the Russia of the 1960's. The Germans then felt, wrongly, or at least for the wrong reasons, deeply humiliated and deprived of the *Lebensraum* they believed they should enjoy. They were eager to reassert their power and to undo the defeat they had suffered in the war. Today, the Russians, by contrast, feel stronger and more highly respected than at any time in their history. Now, for the first time, they are both a great world power and a modern, scientific, industrialized nation. (The Chinese do not enjoy a similar role, and this may explain their very different approach to the international situation.) The Russians do not consider themselves a *Volk ohne Raum,* a people without space. They live, as we Americans do, in a vast, spacious country. Hitler was impatient and inclined to take daring risks; Khrushchev is cautious and has little reason to risk Russia's notable achievements of the past decade on any great gamble of policy. The German people for decades had indulged in the cult of war and militarism, and were even prepared (or so it seemed) to accept the prospect of a Götterdämmerung, of self-destruction for the glory of the fatherland, rather than accept defeat. The Russians, though they have pioneered a vast continent and conquered many peoples (many more than the Germans did), have not glorified war—the praise of peace is a fundamental Russian trait. Different from German *"Kulturpessimismus,"* the Russians are optimistic about the future of man, and thus far removed from a mood of Götterdämmerung.

The enthusiasm for war and the innocence of pre-1914 could never exist today. In those days American Marines were sent to "protect" small countries whenever the United States disapproved of their governments. Today, it is unthinkable that the foremost democratic nation would invade smaller neighboring countries because they were regarded as a threat to American security (as Hitler invaded Czechoslovakia). It would be equally out of the question for the United States to unleash a preventive war, even on a limited scale. The peoples of Europe, from the Channel to the Urals, who have experienced the horrors of two world wars, do not wish to contemplate the coming of another war. Even the Communist nations (save for China and perhaps Albania) now profess to believe that history will bring them their goal without the need of an all-out war. All these factors make it reasonable to expect that there will be no third world war. In 1938, the nations of Asia and Africa played no role in influencing world policy. In the 1960's, they are a factor of growing importance in the United Nations. The election of U Thant, a Burmese Buddhist, as Secretary of the United Nations is no accident; it corresponds to the general trend of the present world revolution. His role is that of mediator; he must try to prevent current world tensions from leading to a holocaust.

The United Nations is of course not an instrument that guarantees harmony and peace; rather it offers the means to assure the coexistence of various civilizations and nations despite their conflicting ideologies and interests. The dream of a unified, harmonious world is as unattainable as the dream of a democratic or a Communist world. The diversity of mankind will continue. This diversity, this pluralism, is a fruitful and creative factor in the evolution of human society. It simply does not make sense to say that the world cannot endure half "free" and half "slave." The world always has been host to both tyranny and freedom. The encouraging thing is that the realm of freedom today is infinitely greater than it has ever been. There are and will always be free nations like Britain, Switzerland, and the United States—as well as others that enjoy much less freedom, such as Communist China, Formosa, Saudi Arabia, Yugoslavia, and Spain. In all probability, freedom in Great Britain, the United States, and Switzerland will remain strong; other countries, like Salazar's Portugal or Gomulka's Poland, much less free today, may in the future gain greater freedom. In other nations, freedom may be sharply diminished, as it was in Italy in the 1920's, in Germany in the 1930's, and in France repeatedly in the nineteenth and twentieth centuries.

All these nations, whatever their heritage of freedom, will meet in the United Nations. There they will discuss their problems and conflicting interests, not necessarily in unity and harmony, but in search of viable compromises. There they will follow the procedures and methods developed over the last centuries by parliamentary government, methods which are those of modern Western civilization. The Western political tradition, the heritage of England and of the Enlightenment, of Locke and Kant, found its expression in the Preamble to the Charter of the United Nations and in the Universal Declaration of Human Rights. They are the fruit of the revolution which began in Western Europe in the second half of the eighteenth century and is today spreading throughout the world at a breathtaking speed. It is difficult for the human mind to adapt itself to such a rapid and profound transformation. Consequently, there may be still more reactions to it, as seen in the nineteenth-century traditionalist movements in France, Germany, and Russia, and then in fascism in our own century. This global revolution is only starting. My generation has been privileged to witness its beginning; it will not live to see its fruition. This is the task, the burden, and, ultimately, the reward of the generations to come.

XVI

A EUROPEAN IN AMERICA

I LEFT SMITH COLLEGE IN 1949 to teach at the City College of New York. I had lived at Northampton for fifteen years—a long time, especially in a life like mine that has experienced so many changes. I made the move because I felt I needed a new environment and new challenges. We lived in apartments on New York's West Side and also in a house in Westchester County; thus I was able to enjoy life in suburbia as well as in the heart of Manhattan. City College, like New York City itself, is a lively, stimulating, and exciting place. The history faculty there, under the chairmanship of Joseph E. Wisan, was an unusually harmonious and happy group. I made many new friends there; since it is impossible to name them all, I will mention only the youngest of them, Wallace Sokolsky, who during my years at City College was my faithful assistant.

There is a great difference between the sheltered, largely self-contained college campus of Smith and the urban university on St. Nicholas Heights in upper Manhattan. The City College campus is situated in West Harlem. Walking to and from the campus I often crossed West Harlem's crowded streets, with their sunny Caribbean

179

flavor, where during good weather life is lived largely outdoors, on the sidewalks and on the steps leading into the
houses. I liked the life in Harlem; for reasons unknown
to me, Negro children seemed closer to nature than white
children, and young Negro men and women seemed taller,
better built, and more graceful than their white counterparts. On the other hand, one could see in Harlem the
misery of slum conditions, as groups of unemployed men
gathered on tenement stoops. There is great tension and
unrest in the Negro quarters of northern cities today; and
now a new pride and determination to improve their lot
are evident among northern Negroes. This is, of course, another aspect of the general world revolution for equality,
and it is one that has become the vital problem in the
United States. The survival of our civilization depends
upon winning this struggle for equality; in the long run, it
is more important than the struggle against communism.

All great cities are full of contrasts, but none as much as
New York City, where (save for Harlem) there is no con-
sistency. Next to a street of elegant luxury apartment
buildings one finds dreary, dilapidated tenements and lofts.
The face of the city and of its various streets is continually
changing. When I first came to know New York, in the
early 1930's, the elevated trains were still running on
Third and Sixth Avenues, and these streets were noisy and
dark. Today, these same streets compete with Fifth and
Park Avenues as sites for luxurious office and apartment
buildings.

There is little reason to lament the passing of the elevated railway, but I do miss the open-top double-decker
buses I used to ride up Riverside Drive and to Fort Tryon
Park; driving along this same route in a car today does
not offer a comparable view of the Palisades across the

wide Hudson River. But buses and public transportation have been downgraded in today's affluent society; every teen-ager now feels he is entitled to his own convertible.

My life in New York was not confined to City College. An urban university and a great metropolitan center provide opportunities to establish contacts in many fields, and contacts and friendships have always been a most important element in my life. Among the men whom I gratefully remember was a Jewish journalist, William Zukerman, who was then in his middle seventies but whose intellectual and physical agility made him appear twenty years younger. In fact, I was deeply astonished to learn, at the time of his death, that he was seventy-six. Until the day before his death he singlehandedly edited the *Jewish Newsletter,* a periodical notable for its insight and courageous stands. It was so much a personal paper that it ended with its editor. It did not speak for any group or party; in an age of self-centered nationalism and conformity, it raised a lonely nonconformist voice and spoke out of an aroused conscience, but not to espouse any ethnic or religious "vital interest." Zukerman stated issues with the sense of objectivity which Hillel demanded as the rule of ethics—an objectivity which tries to understand the motives of the other so that one does not do to others what he does not wish to be done to him. Kant's categorical imperative, of course, reaffirmed this ancient Jewish wisdom.

New York City, more than any other place in the United States—and today more than any other city on earth —is a center of refuge and hence a melting pot. I should like to tell the story of one refugee whom I encountered, the Austrian poet Richard Beer-Hofmann, the friend of Arthur Schnitzler and Hugo von Hofmannsthal. We had often visited with him in Vienna in former days, when his home was that of an art-loving *grand bourgeois*. His was an unusually happy marriage; his wife Paula was a beautiful Austrian woman sixteen years his junior. She tied him even closer to Vienna than did his own upbringing and talent. In those years he wrote to Schnitzler from Italy, "The only city in which I can live and write is Vienna *(ist doch nur Wien)*." When we heard that Beer-Hofmann was now in New York, we looked him up and finally found him, in one of the dismal apartment buildings on New York's West Side. His place was crammed with valuable furniture and art works that he had brought from Europe. He was writing his reminiscences of his life in Austria and of his life with Paula, who had died in Zurich on the way to the United States. He had always written sparingly and with great difficulty; in fact, his total work consists of a few poems, a few plays, and some prose pieces, and fills only a few slender volumes. Now, in New York and in the Catskills, he was writing with greater inspiration and intensity than he ever had in Vienna or Switzerland. With an air of great serenity, the old man, now in his late seventies, recalled for us his happy life. In our many visits with him we found no trace of bitterness. More than ever, though now in the United States, he was the Austrian poet; yet he did not feel uprooted or exiled in a foreign land. "Why should I need roots," he asked, "when I have wings?" (*"Wozu brauche ich denn Wurzeln—ich hab' ja Flügel"*).

In her memoirs, Arthur Schnitzler's widow, Olga Schnitzler, recalls the high spirits of this old man taking up his life again in a new country that was so different from the world of Vienna before 1914—the world in which he and his fellow poets had spent their youth and early man-

hood: "So much is here to learn and to see. Almost everyone has been given an opportunity. Many prejudices are
being thrown overboard; everyone who has not been completely worn out (*jeder nicht völlig Verbrauchte*) experiences here a kind of rebirth. One meets here extraordinary
personalities, for here one can find all kinds of men.
Everyone feels what a grandiose, complex, and broadminded (*grosszügig*) country America is, how well and
free one can live among these people without perfidy and
malice (*Hinterhalt und Tücke*). Yes, we have lost a homeland, but we have gained a world."

Vienna at the beginning of the century was part of the
cultural atmosphere in which I grew up. In recent years I
have tried to recapture the world of its poets and thinkers
in several studies. The capital of the Habsburg empire was
then, much like New York today (though on a much
smaller scale)—a cosmopolitan city and a dynamic intellectual center. Jews played a great role in Vienna, and
nowhere has the cultural vacuum created by Hitlerism left
deeper and more permanent traces than in this once-great
city. The emancipation and assimilation of Jews in Central Europe started with the toleration of the Enlightenment but was never complete, and ended with its barbaric
rejection by German ancestor-centered nationalism. Yet
this assimilation, for all its problems and tensions, greatly
intensified cultural life in Central Europe and made possible the contributions to German and European culture of
very many creative intellects, from Heinrich Heine and
Karl Marx to Sigmund Freud and Arnold Schönberg. Hitlerism put an end to this process of creative assimilation.
To recall and reconstruct this past, the Leo Baeck Institute
has been founded in New York. I have had the pleasure of
working with Max Kreutzberger, its able and dedicated

director. The Institute has succeeded in creating a center for research and publication, connected with similar centers in London (headed by my friend Robert Weltsch) and Jerusalem, and in cooperation with a younger generation of German scholars, all of them trying to preserve the memory of a great period of German and Jewish creative life, a memory which Hitler denigrated and tried to obliterate.

After I moved to New York, some of my "extracurricular" interests were centered less on the past than on the present and the future. In 1954, Robert Strausz-Hupé invited me to become an associate of the Foreign Policy Research Institute of the University of Pennsylvania which he was then establishing. His brilliant mind and his facility of expression attracted me and we became close friends, although his interests lay more in the strategic and military field than mine, and our tastes differed in many ways. My connection with the Institute brought me new friends among my associates there; it also gave me the opportunity to teach courses in the graduate school of the University, which, in many ways, reminded me of Harvard because of its large number of foreign students. Strausz-Hupé and I took a keen interest in the North Atlantic Community; we were instrumental in arranging the Conference on the Community which met at Bruges, Belgium, in September, 1957. The Conference laid its emphasis, not on the military and anticommunist aspects of the North Atlantic Treaty Organization, but on the enduring spiritual and ethical values of modern Western civilization, on the values of an open, free, nonmilitaristic society that offers its heritage of freedom to all mankind.

From 1946 on I have traveled to Europe almost every year, sometimes twice a year. In the wake of the world revolution, Europe itself has changed as much as, if not

more than, Asia and Africa. Since 1946, Europe has risen
from the devastation of war a more beautiful, wealthier,
and happier continent than before. There, too, the process
of equality has made great progress. The European nations and peoples have lost much of their former arrogant
provincialism; they have grown closer together and also
closer to the outside world.

Since sea travel makes me rather uncomfortable, I usually travel by plane. A plane is a great time-saver as well
as a more convenient way of traveling. Some people prefer
the life on shipboard, especially on the great luxury liners
or on cruise ships, but I have never been particularly eager
for such relaxation, and since I do not dance, swim, or
drink, about the only thing I can do on shipboard, namely
reading, I can do much more comfortably at home. Besides, jet planes make it possible for me to go abroad for
a few days' trip to see old friends and to make new ones,
particularly with younger people, and to participate in
conferences.

The number of international conferences of all kinds
has increased rapidly in recent years. Such conferences
seem to me productive, both in stimulating contacts and in
the exchange of knowledge, if they are kept to manageable
size. I took an active part in the International Congress of
Historical Sciences in Rome (1955) and in Stockholm
(1960), in the Congress of the International Association
of Political Science in Paris (1961), and in three conferences arranged by the Congress for Cultural Freedom
in Hamburg (1953), Milan (1955), and Berlin (1960),
as well as in the celebration of the tenth anniversary of
NATO in London (1959). Perhaps such international
conferences should not be held in metropolitan centers,
which do offer too many distractions; and perhaps they

should be limited in size so that a real dialogue of ideas is possible. I have attended small conferences, and found them always truly rewarding. I have already mentioned the Bruges Conference. The International Society for the History of Ideas, which I founded with my friend Philip Wiener, held such a conference at Peterhouse, Cambridge, England, in September, 1960, and another even smaller conference on Nationalism and Mankind met in 1961 at the lovely Villa Serbelloni above Lake Como. There were Americans, Europeans, Asians, and Africans meeting in the most stimulating exchange it was ever my privilege to listen to.

I have also frequently taught and lectured in Europe for short periods after World War II. Because of my background and the postwar situation, most of these lectures have been delivered in Germany. Since only the "right" people come to hear me, my reception on the whole has been very friendly. I find the German problem a very complex one. I am convinced that it is wrong to see in the present German Federal Republic a bastion of reaction or militarism. Bonn is neither the Second Reich nor the Weimar Reich. Naturally, there are still Germans, especially among the older generation, who look back nostalgically upon Bismarck and the period of German hegemony and do not recognize it as a disastrous turning point in German history. Many of these Germans also believe that the United States should not have fought Hitler, but rather should have recognized the righteousness of Germany's cause in fighting communism and supported Hitler's effort to "save" European civilization. These people forget that fascism in Europe was a greater threat to civilization than communism; that Hitler's regime surpassed Stalin's in stark barbarism. It was Hitler who destroyed conservative Catholic Poland as a buffer protecting Europe from communism. They forget that it was Hitler who concluded a treaty of friendship and nonaggression with the Soviet Union, and then broke it in an act of wanton aggression that led directly to the Russian invasion of Central Europe. They forget that it was Hitler who declared war upon the United States and thus brought this nation into war against Germany. (Even today some Germans regard Franklin D. Roosevelt, not Hitler, as the villain of recent history.)

Happily, many young Germans born in the 1920's and early 1930's have a genuine love of freedom; in fact, this generation is the most liberal and cosmopolitan German generation since the Enlightenment. They have learned from history, they understand the roots of National Socialism in past German attitudes, and they wish to lay strong foundations for a life of liberty, *eine freiheitliche Lebensordnung,* in Germany. In contrast to the development of German antidemocratic and anti-Western attitudes in the decades after the 1860's, the strength of democracy among German youth today is gratifying.

No one wishes to deny that a residue of authoritarianism still survives in public and in personal life in the German Federal Republic. But the point to remember is that compared with the German governments of the past, the Republic at Bonn represents real progress and promise. Once before, in 1848, there was a similar democratic stirring in Germany; but it was a naïve hope, brutally crushed by Prussian arms. Today there is much greater hope for a stable democracy in Germany, and there are no Prussian troops to threaten its extinction. The present German government and Austria's democratic regime (maintained since 1945 by the coalition of Catholic Conservatives and

Social Democrats) are among the most significant and hopeful developments in the postwar world. I have become quite optimistic about the future of these nations after many visits to contemporary Germany and Austria, particularly when I compare them with the Weimar Reich, when Bismarckism and Prussianism were so easily revived, or with the First Austrian Republic, when conservative authoritarianism quickly destroyed liberty.

My travels abroad have not interfered with my work in the United States. Perhaps it is human nature, but when I am in the United States I sometimes long to go abroad; at the same time, when I am abroad I always long to return to the States, to my desk, to my students. I include among "students" all my audiences. Among my adult audiences I have been most impressed with the students at the great military schools where I have often lectured. Their exposure to civilian thought and to a variety of viewpoints is virtually unknown in Europe. I first lectured to such an audience in 1939, at the Naval War College at Newport, Rhode Island. I especially remember my frequent visits there in 1946, 1947, and 1948, with Admiral Raymond Spruance, then president of the College. Spruance had distinguished himself as wartime Commander of the Fifth Task Force in the Pacific, and he impressed me as a gentle man of rare humanity and a scholarly nature. The audiences at all American military colleges are carefully selected; they consist of unusually well-informed and thoughtful men of wide experience, well grounded in history and geography. The lecturer does not encounter there the uniformity of attitudes that he might expect but rather he finds open and receptive minds that entertain all attitudes and interpretations honestly set forth.

Most people everywhere like to hear lectures which

confirm their opinions; yet lectures should present new and challenging viewpoints and contradict widely accepted assumptions and interpretations. Good lectures should arouse a critical awareness of the complex motivations underlying political actions. Lectures in contemporary history and political science render a service by presenting "heretical" points of view, though such viewpoints should be presented as hypotheses and in the knowledge that other interpretations are also possible. I have always tried to follow this rule as far as I could, though I have not always succeeded. Much depends on the stimulation generated by the audience's reaction. I was fortunate in finding such receptive audiences frequently in American universities and military schools.

XVII

WIDENING HORIZON
AND NEW HOPES

THUS THE YEARS PASSED, and I reached the age of seventy. It is ancient wisdom, banal but nevertheless true, that old age comes as a surprise. *"Eheu fugaces labuntur anni"* ("Ah me, the fleeting years are slipping by"), Horace mourned. Two thousand years later Italo Svevo, a Triestino author, made the same point. A few months before he died in 1928, in a motorcar accident, at the age of sixty-seven, he wrote in his diary: "In my bungled life I do not understand that something as serious as growing old could happen to me. Old age introduces itself by minutes which grow into hours which grow into days."

At seventy I had to retire from City College. The department and the students were more generous than I expected or deserved in expressing their appreciation of our cooperation and friendship. Nonetheless, I resented, not so much the fact of age itself, which is inevitable, but the fact of compulsory retirement. Men in more difficult positions—justices of the Supreme Court or members of Congress—can go on as long as their mental and physical strength allows. And I had looked forward to participating in a new stage of growth for City College; then just as it began I had to leave. Because I had started so late in the teaching profession, my retirement pension was less than a sixth of my regular salary, far below a minimum subsistence level. So at the age of seventy-one I again started on years of *Wanderschaft,* to continue my work and to earn my living.

We gave up our residence in New York; my wife went along gladly, as she had gone along when I decided to give up my position in Palestine and set out on the uncertain road of *Wanderschaft* thirty years ago. The loss of a home hurt her more, of course, than it hurt me. But she adapted courageously to the life of provisional arrangements and permanent valises. We gave away most of our books and furniture; the rest was stored. And so far the experience of our new *Wandershaft* has been a happy one. We spent 1962 at the Social Science Foundation of the University of Denver, which is expanding rapidly, under the able and dedicated leadership of Josef Korbel, a former Czech diplomat. We were received with great friendliness, made new friends, and enjoyed the climate that the Denverites rightly boast about. This year we are back in New England, in the Center for Advanced Studies at Wesleyan University, which my late friend Sigmund Neumann helped to establish. I had looked forward to working wtih him; now he, though younger than I, has gone before me. How long the *Wanderjahre* will last and where they will lead us, I do not know, but I am greatful for the chances to start anew. Chances and changes: When one is confronted by new tasks, new horizons, and new challenges, life goes on, and a person, no matter what his age, goes on with them. As long as one is privileged to begin anew, one is in the midst of life. My father died—to come back where I began—a traveling salesman in his seventy-sixth year in a provincial railroad station, ready after a day's good work to board the train for home. Only I have no "home" in the accepted bourgeois sense, though my need for one is not so great as my father's was.

My generation has witnessed so many dramatic changes and passed through so many profound crises that its life has, indeed, been long and full. I took part in many of these changes, and suffered in many of its crises, as is the human predicament. Now in old age I have learned to look with some detachment, tolerance, and even serenity on my own shortcomings (and those of others) and on the troubles that life brings. Some of life's incidents were bitter ones, difficult to accept at the time. Yet *"forsan et hanc meminisse juvabit"* ("this too will be helpful when remembered"), and so my present trials have lost much of their bitterness through the acceptance which old age imposes. At this stage of life, which I have now reached, it may not appear presumptuous if one states one's "credo," one's belief about life in general and about one's own time, as briefly and simply as it may be possible.

"La vita è burla" ("Life is a farce"), the octogenarian Verdi proclaimed in *Falstaff*. To many men, their own life has seemed in vain and their times out of joint. I have always been attracted to the inscriptions on old tombstones, which sometimes sum up a life in a few words or lines better than a whole novel or personal confession might. Visiting an old churchyard in England in the 1850's, Hawthorne discovered such an inscription and after his return to the United States wrote about it in *Our Old Home*. He observed "that one of the gravestones lay very close to the church—so close that the droppings of the eaves would fall upon him. It seemed as if the in-

mate of that grave had desired to creep under the church-wall. On closer inspection, we found an almost illegible epitaph on the stone, and with difficulty made out this for-lorn verse:

> Poorly lived,
> And poorly died,
> Poorly buried,
> And no one cried.

It would be hard to compress the story of a cold and luck-less life, death and burial into fewer words, or more im-pressive ones; at least, we found them impressive, perhaps because we had to re-create the inscription by scraping away the lichens from the faintly traced letters. . . . His name, as well as I could make it out, was Treeo—John Treeo, I think—and he died in 1810, at the age of seventy-four. The gravestone is so overgrown with grass and weeds, and so crumbly with time and foul weather, that it is questionable whether anybody will ever be at the trouble of deciphering it again. But there is a quaint and sad enjoyment in defeating (to such slight degree as my pen may do it) the probabilities of oblivion for poor John Treeo, and asking a little sympathy for him, half a century after his death, and making him better and more widely known, at least, than any other slumberer in Lillington churchyard: he having been, as appearances go, the out-cast of them all."

No one knows of Treeo's family or circumstances, yet there was Wolfgang von Goethe, Goethe's younger grand-son, who had lived his childhood in Germany's most dis-tinguished home and died in 1883 at the height of Ger-many's dynamic growth. He left the following short poem:

Ich stehe stets daneben,
Ich trete niemals ein.
Ich möchte einmal leben,
Ich möchte einmal sein.

I always stand aside,
I never enter.
Once I would like to live,
Once I would like to be.

This melancholy summing-up can be matched by that of a man who was no recluse like Goethe's grandson, but a highly gifted and unusually brilliant American *grand seigneur,* a man of the great world, widely traveled and widely learned, Henry Adams. From Nürnberg on August 3, 1901—the century was then very young, confident, and hopeful, and Adams not yet old, just sixty-two years—he wrote: "All together, Germany gives me the sense of hopeless failure. In fact, I have had more than enough of Europe altogether, and I am afraid my appetite for America is not voracious either. The world has lived too long. So have I. One of us two has got to go. For the public good, it had better be the world that goes. For at least I am harmless."

William Butler Yeats, whom I consider the greatest twentieth-century poet of the English language, like Goethe and Ibsen, wrote some of his most enduring works after he had reached sixty; nevertheless, he prayed in old age

That I may seem, though I die old,
A foolish passionate man,

and bitterly complained.

What shall I do with this absurdity—
O heart, O troubled heart—this caricature,
Decrepit age, that has been tied to me
As to a dog's tail.

From the land of youth and love, he wished to sail to
Byzantium and pray to the sages standing at God's holy
fire:

Consume my heart away; sick with desire
And fastened to a dying animal
It knows not what it is; and gather me
Into the artifice of eternity.

That life is difficult and earnest, there is no doubt.
"Ars longa, vita brevis" means not only that life is short
and art is long to learn but also that one never arrives at
the end of learning. This predicament is even more true
of the most difficult art of all, an art never well enough
learned: the art of how to live as a human being and how
to live together with other, very different human beings.

No one escapes the tragic character of life. By its nature, its finiteness and finality, life dictates ultimate frustration. One rarely catches glimpses of the end of the road
to be traveled and even more rarely does he have the feeling of reaching it. Outward obstacles may be partly responsible for this frustration, but in life I have found the
inner obstacles more important. Ovid expressed this attitude very succinctly when he wrote: *"Video meliora pro-
boque, deteriora sequor"* ("I see what is better and I approve of it, and yet I follow what is worse").

Pessimism and the deprecation of man's life have been
pervasive attitudes throughout history, not only in an age

when "God is dead," but perhaps even more in ages of faith. During the Middle Ages, one of the seven deadly sins was *acedia,* or *accidie.* The word means "not caring for" or "not concerned with" and signifies a state of spiritual torpor or apathy, an extreme state of despair and indifference. Acedia does not mean "overcoming" life and its anxieties in the way of Buddhist enlightenment, but a hopeless drowning in a life without values, aspirations, or meaning. Today again one notes a trend toward viewing man's fate and existence as one of continuous, inherent anxiety and loneliness lived in the shadow of death. This view seems to prevail among Western intellectuals—but not among the masses, and certainly not among non-Western peoples. I do not share this feeling. Naturally, from the hour of birth, when we emerge from nonexistence, we are beginning to die and are moving toward that moment when we shall go back to nonexistence. There have always been those who could not bear this thought. Yet between inception, birth, and infancy, and the often painful approach of death, there are years which man can fill with beauty and things of meaning to him and to others, and man has done so all during his history.

Many people, at one time or another, come to feel that life has lost significance. This is understandable and usually is a passing thing. But since the two world wars a kind of permanent alienation from life seems to have become a fairly widespread phenomenon. The extremes of the human condition—especially the fact that all men are alone in the face of death—have begun to be regarded as "normal" and normative, determining all our life. A willing commitment to life, with all its risks and despair, to many men appears a sign of shallow superficiality or bourgeois obtuseness. Supposedly, this is the "modern" predicament; yet the means of escape many have chosen is a primitive hedonism, just as in primitive times escape from life was found in sensual pleasure, in cruelty, in domination.

In his prophetic, though one-sided, analysis of our age and of his personal situation, Nietzsche foresaw the coming of the era of "nihilism." Yet despite sickness and loneliness—real sickness and real loneliness—Nietzsche affirmed life and hope and the possibility of human endurance and human greatness. Throughout his life, Nietzsche remained faithful to one man and took him as his ideal, Goethe. In Nietzsche's last book, *The Twilight of the Idols,* he wrote of Goethe as a superman, as what he himself hoped to become and what he expected that man might become: "He did not desert life, but placed himself at its center. He was not fainthearted but took as much as possible upon himself, into himself. What he aimed at was wholeness; he fought against separating reason from sensuality, feeling, will. He disciplined himself into wholeness, he created himself. He envisaged man as strong, highly civilized, graceful in every gesture, self-controlled, having respect for himself as a creature who might dare to afford the whole range and wealth of being natural, of being strong enough for such freedom, the man of tolerance, not from weakness but from strength, because he knows how to use to his advantage what would destroy an average person. Such a mind, having attained real freedom, lives in the very center of all things with a joyful and confident acceptance of fate, lives in the faith that . . . in the wholeness of life everything is affirmed and redeemed. He no longer negates."

Nietzsche lacked Goethe's spontaneous sense of measure and balance, and succumbed to what he called "the

magic power of extremes." But he rightly pointed out that
Goethe did not share the fashionable view of the roman-
ticists of his own age (a view even more fashionable today) that the great artist must be unhappy and lonely and
that success stories belong to the "bourgeois" world.
Goethe was a favorite of the gods, a *Götterliebling,* not
because he produced immortal work—Michelangelo,
Shakespeare, and Beethoven equaled him in this regard—
but because he mastered the art of living, the most difficult art to learn (his first important biographer, Carl Gustav Carus, called it *Lebenskunst*). Goethe suffered greatly
in body and mind; he underwent, even in old age, profound emotional crises which threatened to destroy him.
But he controlled his passion and overcame infirmities,
sorrows, and dangers; unbroken and unbowed, working
and striving till the very end, he could tell us, like Ten-
nyson's Ulysses, "It's not too late to seek a newer world."
Goethe had confidence in nature and in life. To quote
Wolfgang Leppmann, man, to Goethe, was not, as he was
for Kierkegaard, Strindberg, or Kafka, "essentially out of
step with the world in which he finds himself."

Johannes Urzidil has aptly entitled his study of Goethe's
relationship with the United States *Das Glück der Gegen-
wart* (*The Happiness of the Present*). The old man's loving admiration had less to do with America's material
achievements than with its moral foundations and its climate of individual liberty, equal opportunity, and broad
tolerance. In his seventy-seventh year, Goethe wrote a
poem about America and spoke of *"des edlen Landes
Glück"* ("the happiness of the noble land"), stressing that
in that nation "the earth is set free through love and that
through deeds it grows great."

> Die Erde wird durch Liebe frei,
> Durch Taten wird sie gross.

In one of the poems from *West-Oestlicher Divan,* a great book of his old age, the poet answers the complaint that "the advancing years took so much away from him"— *"Die Jahre nahmen mir, du sagst, so vieles"*—with the words *"Mir bleibt genug! Es bleibt Idee und Liebe!"* ("There is so much left to me; there are ideas, and love.") These words were inspired by Goethe's love for Marianne von Willemer, and by her love for him.

Ibsen, the greatest dramatist of modern times, was not a favorite of the gods as was Goethe. Both were more popular in their earlier works, but both reached their full mastership at an advanced age. Like his earlier works, Ibsen's last plays dealt with the individual's faithfulness to himself, his self-realization, his growth through self-discipline. At the same time and with ever greater insistence, these plays asked hard questions about the substance and meaning of life—whether man lived his life, whether old age brought fulfillment or despair. In Rebecca West and Hilda Wangel, Ibsen introduced the challenge, the temptation, and the promise with which youth confronts age. Rosmer and Solness were too weak to stand the challenge of youth as Goethe had. The two women—in their youthful strength, descendants of the Vikings—did not bring a renewed creative power to the older men, but came as Valkyries announcing death.

In his last play *When We Dead Awaken,* Ibsen asked whether his life was not a failure, in spite of outward success and apparent achievement. The great artist questioned his own work and came to disassociate life and art. He believed that in his dedication to his work he had missed living his life. Looking back upon a career which had brought him acclaim, honor, and wealth, he found it a stretch of emptiness from which life had fled. Goethe, to whom work was indissolubly part of life, would not have understood such a dilemma.

But as against the melancholy self-doubt of his last play, Ibsen gave a stronger and more affirmative answer in his preceding play, in many ways his greatest. Its hero, John Gabriel Borkman, remains faithful to the very end to what he has regarded as his calling and vocation. In spite of outward catastrophe and loneliness, he does not abandon hope nor see his life as meaningless, but triumphantly reasserts its dream and drive. The play ends on two levels which contrast and yet unite old age and youth, the tragic final reckoning, in pride or resignation, with life and the comedy of the hopeful anticipation of life. At the top of the hill, Borkman dies unbroken and unbowed in the icy wintry night, and two old women, twin sisters who had fought a bitter feud for this man all their life, clasp hands over his dead body, for the first time in so many years. Meanwhile, in the valley below, unaware of the tragedy and caring little about the fate of the old man, three young people in a sleigh with ringing silver bells escape to southern lands, to sunshine and joy. In spite of Ibsen's reticence about himself, one feels that the old poet's heart is with youth and its unconcerned, even ruthless, forsaking of old age, that he realistically accepts what seems the cruelty of life and draws comfort from the ever-renewed promise of spring and a new beginning.

Goethe and Ibsen were not the only guideposts in my life who turned me away from the fashionable despair of my contemporaries. The poet of my younger years, Rainer

Maria Rilke, knew as well as any other poet the immi-
nence of death, the loneliness of life, the impenetrable
mystery of living. Death, of course, forms the very center
of his *Sonnets to Orpheus,* the death which takes us before we have learned the lessons of life:

> Nicht sind die Leiden erkannt,
> Nicht ist die Liebe gelernt,
> Und was im Tod uns entfernt
> Ist nicht entschleiert.

Rilke knew that "the sufferings are not understood, love
has not been learned, and what removes us in death has
not been unveiled." Yet he did not give way to despair
and lament. In his *Notebook of Malte Laurids Brigge,*
perhaps the most devastating document of human loneliness in a great city, the grotesque misery of Paris haunts
the reader as powerfully as it does in Baudelaire's *Flowers
of Evil.* But after finishing the book, Rilke commented: "I
am just now more one-sided than ever; the lament has
prevailed, but I know that one should use the chords of
lament only if one is determined also to play on them
later the whole jubilation, which grows behind everything
that is heavy, painful, and endured, and without which
the voices are not complete." Ten years later, Rilke wrote
to a young man bewildered by life that "the taking of life
seriously, of which my books are full, has nothing to do
with melancholy. . . . It does not wish to be anything else
but taking life as it truly is . . . no rejection, on the contrary, how much infinite assent, and ever-renewed assent
to existence!" Rilke's last poems voiced that assent to
life and death which the young man could not yet reach.
Though conscious of all the anxiety, of all the absurdi-

ties of life, the poet defined his vocation and work as
"rühmen" (to praise) in a poem, which in Jessie Lamont's
translation begins,

> O tell us, Poet, what you do?—
>   I praise.
> But the dark, the deadly, the desperate ways,
> How do you endure them—how bear them?—
>   I praise.

The example of poets has helped me to assent hopefully
to man's fate in my time. But an even more influential
factor has been my increasing understanding of the history
I experienced in the last half-century and my appreciation
of the unique world revolution through which I have been
living. The world revolution I am referring to is not, primarily, the technical and scientific revolution of our age,
though, of course, I do not underrate its importance. Man
is, indeed, conquering space and annihilating distance today; age-old dreams, which were man's flights of fancy
or fairy tales in other eras, have been realized in my lifetime. Today, young people regard a plane flight of a few
hours from New York to Paris, Baghdad, and Tokyo as
commonplace. This is quite natural, since they have never
known it otherwise; indeed, their children may, in turn, regard flights to the planets as equally commonplace. The
dark side of the moon may be as familiar to the next
generation as the "dark" continent of Africa has become
to young people today. Space will yield its secrets as the
earth has. But time will not. Its irrevocability is its unique
characteristic. One can recross oceans and deserts many
times; he can never relive the past. One can never know
the future, but only help to build it.

Revolutionary times are hopeful times. The winds of the future billow the sails of mankind's ship. But these winds can become destructive gales, and humanity's ship can flounder on the seas of fanaticism and hatred. Such was the fate of the Russian Revolution. It was a revolution narrowed by Russia's traditional authoritarianism; it was based on class war and bitter hatred; it was hostile to accommodation, contemptuous of its opponents and of traditional international morality. Thus the great hope aroused in November, 1917, dissolved in dismal failure, climaxed by the Stalinist terror. By contrast, the world revolution since 1945 has many hopeful aspects, in spite of the horrors of Hiroshima, the Algerian bloodbath, and fratricidal Asian wars. This is a universal revolution and it is proceeding with less violence than might have been expected. In the West, it marks the transition from nineteenth-century capitalism, with its survivals of rigid class distinctions, to modern capitalism, with its equality of opportunity and fluidity of class barriers. In Asia and Africa, it marks the transition from colonialism to independence, from dominion to equality of status. And finally, throughout the world, it marks the transition from a European-centered and European-led globe to an ecumenical order in which all civilizations and people meet for the first time in common intercourse and common efforts. All these revolutionary transformations have been set in motion in a few short years; they have occurred with greater smoothness than anyone could have expected. On the whole, this revolution has been progressing in a spirit of accommodation never before seen during a great turning point of history.

This hopeful and beneficent revolution in the new social order of the West, in the new political order in Asia and

Africa has resulted in the emergence for the first time in history of a common mankind. This revolution has been the principal fact of the twentieth century. And this revolution has not witnessed the collapse of Western civilization nor the breakdown of the capitalist system, as the prophets of doom predicted a few decades ago; nor has there been any challenge to Western civilization by new barbarian peoples; in any event, the major manifestations of modern barbarism have been among the so-called civilized nations of Europe. The much-abused parallel between our age and the collapse of the Roman Empire, with the long night of civilization that followed it, has not been confirmed by events.

From our encounter with the history of the last half-century we have also learned to distrust utopian hopes. The Communist Revolution has failed dismally; it did not bring greater human liberty nor solve the problems of economic productivity. Fascism too, despite its arrogant assertion that it would create a "nobler" man by reverting to pre-Enlightenment morality and the premise of human inequality has been proven wrong. Even Gandhi was unable to leave his people a heritage fundamentally different from the newly emergent nationalism of other peoples.

These few examples demonstrate clearly that human nature does not change fundamentally. The utopian hopes of the French Revolution, and of its many disciples from Fichte to Marx, have, in fact, imperiled the transformation of human and social relationships since the Enlightenment. Marx described communism as the "definitive resolution of the antagonism between man and nature, and between man and man. [It] is the true solution of the conflict . . . between freedom and necessity, between individual and species. It is the solution of the riddle of history and knows itself to be this solution."

No such definite solution of the antagonisms and tensions in human life and society is possible. Neither religion nor communism has achieved it. Any such utopian hope, whether based on religious faith, on social revolution, or on scientific progress, can only end in frustration and failure. The absolute good is as unattainable as the perfect harmony of family life, or of national or international society. Man can only hope to ameliorate troubled conditions and prevent them from leading to open conflict and disaster. But tensions and conflicts will remain—part of the innate imperfection of man—as will the differences of temperament, character, and interests among peoples and civilizations. Yet today relations between the peoples of the world are somewhat better than they were before 1914 or before 1945, even though they are still far from satisfactory. We have learned to put greater store in the dignity of the individual of all races and classes, and to show greater regard for human life, greater compassion for the infirm and unfortunate, the disinherited and oppressed, than at any time since the Enlightenment. True, much of this remains lip-service, but in most of man's past not even lip-service was paid to these principles; thus an important first step has been made on this difficult road. For the vast majority of mankind, life is becoming easier and more meaningful than ever before.

Many of those who tend to praise the past inordinately bewail what appears to them the immorality of our time. Though sex was much less openly discussed in past eras than it is today, adultery, polygamy, prostitution, and promiscuity were probably as widespread even in the ages of faith and of religious conformity as they are today.

As far as I can observe, many young people today lead lives of strict "Victorian" morality, though they do it with greater awareness and joy than the Victorians did. It is also significant that the great emancipators of modern times—Ibsen and Mill, Nietzsche and Freud, Marx and Lenin—were almost puritanical in their personal morals, even though their morality was not based on obedience to any religious rule or socially dictated ethic. Paradoxically, the lives of these modern "immoralists" were, in many ways, as "saintly" as those of the few truly saintly members of religious organizations. The new liberty, as Ibsen stressed, does not imply a relaxation of the code of morality but rather an enhanced feeling of individual responsibility.

The complaint about the moral decay alleged against our society is a very ancient one. It is contained, with the same intensity, in the pages of Chinese and Egyptian scholars several thousand years ago, in the words of the Hebrew prophets, in the writings of classical Greece and Rome, of the Middle Ages, and of modern times. People who lack historical perspective tend to lament the dissolution of their own society as if it presented them with a singular spectacle of depravity; they look longingly to an imagined nobler past, or envision a roseate future of perfected humanity. But this age-old lament of the depravity of one's own times, especially complaints about the conduct of the younger generation, only bears out the universality of certain human or ethical values. The more highly developed civilizations throughout the ages have always formulated an image of how man ought to live, a concept of the meaning of life, which defies precise definition yet is generally understood and accepted. Without this tacitly accepted norm, complaints about the decline of morality make no sense, for they must be premised on the existence of such a norm. Of course, such a standard of conduct varies greatly among civilizations in different ages; yet in all of them there has been a certain uniformity in what man regards as right and good, as the ideal norm of the *homo humanus,* as the basic objectives of mankind—though he may fail to live up to them.

Our age is not more immoral than any other. In many respects, it is more deeply human and humane. It has become more and more distrustful of radical solutions, of panaceas to transform human nature and society; it acknowledges more clearly the difficulties of human intercourse and the stubborn strength of prejudice; it is learning patience; it is becoming less parochial and more universal. All these trends are seen clearly in the United Nations, which itself is one of the most important mirrors of the worldwide revolution of our time. The General Assembly that met in the fall of 1962 was presided over by a Pakistani Moslem, and it elected a Burmese Buddhist as Secretary General. In his acceptance speech, U Thant emphasized this new spirit of our times. "When the future of mankind itself is at stake, no country or interest-group can afford to take a rigid stand, or claim that its position is the only right one, and that others must take or leave it. No difficult problem can be solved to the complete satisfaction of all sides. We live in an imperfect world, and have to accept imperfect solutions, which become more acceptable as we learn to live with them and as time passes by."

It is a sign of our times that today an Asian speaks the language of modern Western civilization—a language of faith in man's ability to control his basic passions, of patient acceptance of human shortcomings, of mutual open-minded tolerance—the same language which Dag Hammarskjöld would have spoken.

The West continues to reflect the strength of its spiritual heritage, too. No document is as significant in this respect as the encyclical *"Pacem in terris"* ("Peace on Earth") of Pope John XXIII. The thoughtful observer must compare it with the *"Syllabus errorum"* ("Syllabus of Errors") of Pope Pius IX promulgated one hundred years ago (1864) to measure the road traveled. Of course, the atmosphere of the Cold War caused some observers to interpret Pope John's deeply moving document as an unwise step toward an accommodation with communism—despite the fact that it emanated from the oldest and most tradition-bound spokesman for the Western world. But history will regard it as infinitely more: It is a great document in the West's (and mankind's) long ascent to greater freedom and its dedication to the dignity of man. The gates of the Church have been opened to the modern world, to the world-community of man, and to the spirit of justice and liberty.

"Pacem in terris" speaks not only to Catholics, but to Protestants, Jews, Moslems, and Buddhists, to agnostics and atheists. It is a truly catholic appeal to mankind, for freedom, tolerance, and peace, an unprecedented affirmation of concern for all mankind by the head of the Universal Church. The Ecumenical Council called at the Vatican by Pope John XXIII, and reconvened by his successor, Paul VI, was inspired by a spirit very different from that of the first Vatican Council called by Pope Pius IX a century ago. The new Council has borne witness to the world revolution which has occurred in our postwar era. The encyclical has made it clear that the Vatican no longer identifies the Church with the outmoded regimes of the past, with political authoritarianism, with the denial of

liberty of thought, religion, and conscience; that it no longer identifies the Church with Europe, with European domination and European interests. The Church, for the first time, has spoken out on behalf of all of mankind.

Many thoughtful persons feared a cultural decline of the West in the postwar era, but, happily, they were wrong. Those who continue to see a corruption in our cultural standards do so out of a lack of historical perspective. It is true that mediocre and untalented writers, for example, are more widely read today than good authors, but that has been the case throughout history. In his lifetime, Kotzebue was much more popular with the public, and sold many more copies of his works, than his contemporary, Goethe. Though students seldom study Greek today, the fact is that books on Greek culture and literature are now more widely read than was the case fifty or one hundred years ago. In American colleges interest in the classics is growing; hundreds of thousands of copies of books about ancient Greece and Rome are sold in paperback editions. And translations of the classics published in the United States today are far better than the older European translations. In 1962 the University of Texas began to publish a quarterly, *Arion,* a journal of imaginative criticism of the classics which tries to interpret the classics for the present generation as living literature. Records and FM radio make available the finest music of all periods to a much wider public than ever before. While the West studies Oriental and African music and sculpture, the East learns to master Western techniques in all the arts. This growing cultural community of mankind would have seemed a fanciful ideal that could never be realized just a few decades ago, when I was young.

In this growing political and cultural community of

mankind, differences among national civilizations and religions will not disappear. Their national past and traditions will continue to influence peoples' behavior and attitudes. Within the European cultural community of the nineteenth century, the literatures of Russia and Spain, of England and France, of Scandinavia and Italy preserved their distinctive national character and influenced each other. In the emerging world literature, which Goethe foresaw one hundred and fifty years ago, nationalism will express itself in a similar way, as it will in the political style, in the way of life of the various peoples.

Almost half a century ago I began studying nationalism. At that time few scholars in the English-speaking countries paid much attention to the vital importance of this central phenomenon of our times. Professor Carlton J. H. Hayes of Columbia University pioneered in this field in the United States. Today, the significance of the study of nationalism is widely recognized. Much excellent work has been done by younger scholars, including my colleague Louis L. Snyder and the late Koppel S. Pinson. The impact of nationalism on mankind will remain a major concern of statesmen and scholars for a long time to come. The "nation-state" and "mankind" originated as ideas in the minds of men. Since then nations and nationalism have grown into commanding realities throughout the earth, and "mankind" is slowly emerging as a reality in the present decade. It is one of the main aspects of the great revolution through which we are passing today.

The words I quoted from U Thant gain significance just because they are expressed by a representative of one of the newly emerging nations. They sum up what I have learned from my encounters with history during the past half-century, during the first worldwide revolution in man's relationship with man. Some of this spirit of good will and tolerance, of moderation and compromise, characterized the last decades of the Austria where I spent my youth. Then, as today, many conflicts and tensions existed, and self-righteousness made solutions difficult. Then, as today, no panacea, no perfect solution existed, least of all in a recourse to war. But the statesmen of my day would not tolerate a compromise solution. The patient quest for such a solution was abandoned in favor of the total solutions that could only be gained by war, and so began an era of nationalist extremism and crusading ideologies. Man's recourse to arms did not improve things, however. The solutions dictated by the war were transitory, many of them contrary to the true interests of the victors and vanquished alike. Is it too much to hope that the new spirit developing out of the world revolution of our time will produce more lasting results that will benefit mankind?

A bibliography of Hans Kohn's books published between 1922 and 1963 will be found on pages 357 to 360 of his *REFLECTIONS ON MODERN HISTORY* (Princeton, New Jersey: D. Van Nostrand Co., Inc., 1963).